Jesus

Michael Keene

LION
ACCESS
GUIDES

Copyright © 2002 Michael Keene
This edition copyright © 2002 Lion
Publishing

The author asserts the moral right
to be identified as the author of this work

Published by
Lion Publishing plc
Mayfield House, 256 Banbury Road,
Oxford OX2 7DH, England
www.lion-publishing.co.uk
ISBN 0 7459 5066 3

First edition 2002
10 9 8 7 6 5 4 3 2 1 0

All rights reserved

A catalogue record for this book is
available from the British Library

Typeset in 10.25/11 Venetian 301
Printed and bound in China

Text acknowledgments
The scripture quotations contained herein
are from The New Revised Standard
Version of the Bible, Anglicized Edition,
copyright © 1989, 1995 by the Division
of Christian Education of the National
Council of the Churches of Christ in the
United States of America, and are used by
permission. All rights reserved.
Scriptures quoted from the Good News
Bible are published by The Bible Societies/
HarperCollins Publishers Ltd, UK ©
American Bible Society 1966, 1971, 1976,
1992, and used with permission.
Scripture quotations taken from the *Holy
Bible, New International Version*, copyright ©
1973, 1978, 1984 by International Bible
Society. Used by permission of Hodder &
Stoughton Limited. All rights reserved.
'NIV' is a registered trademark of

International Bible Society. UK trademark
number 1448790.

Picture acknowledgments
Please see page 160.

Contents

Note
Throughout this
series the convention
is followed of dating
events by the
abbreviations BCE
(Before Common Era)
and CE (Common
Era). They correspond
precisely to the more
familiar BC and AD.

Introducing Jesus

Jesus Christ is perhaps the most influential person in history. He was born, lived and died in Palestine, on the edge of the Roman empire, and spent only about three years in the public eye. His legacy was to lay the foundations on which Christianity was built and to create followers throughout the world.

For over 2,000 years Jesus of Nazareth has been a pivotal figure in human history. During this time the Christian religion, built on his life and teaching, has drawn untold numbers into accepting him as the Son of God and Saviour of the world. Today the number of Christians scattered throughout the world probably exceeds two billion – 30 per cent of the total world population.

Most of what we know about Jesus of Nazareth comes from the four Gospels in the New Testament. Two of them, Matthew and Luke, tell us that Jesus was born in Bethlehem, an event that took place in 5/4 BCE.

Bethlehem was a small village in Palestine, a tiny country on the eastern fringe of the Roman empire and no larger than 13,000 square kilometres. The million or so Jews who lived there had fallen under Roman domination in 63 BCE and had not enjoyed a day of freedom since. They desperately longed for the coming of the Messiah, the deliverer who had been promised to them in their scriptures. Many of them hoped, for a short time, that Jesus was the God-given answer to their prayers.

Jesus grew up in the town of Nazareth and worked with his father as a carpenter until John the Baptist, his cousin, began his preaching and baptizing ministry on the banks of the River Jordan. One day Jesus emerged from the crowd of onlookers, was baptized by John and began his public ministry, probably in 29 CE. We do not know how long this ministry lasted since the Gospel-writers have not left us many chronological clues, but most scholars of the New Testament believe that it lasted between one and three years.

During that time Jesus healed the sick and trained his 12 chosen disciples to continue his work, but right from the start he seemed to sense that his ministry was going to be short-lived. To begin with, the people responded to the unique authority of his teaching, but Jesus soon made many enemies from among the different religious groups operating in Palestine at the time. These enemies plotted his death and successfully arranged his arrest and trial before Pontius Pilate, the Roman governor, the only person in Palestine with the authority to pass the death sentence. Once passed the sentence was speedily carried out and Jesus died in 30 or 31 CE.

The story did not end there. The Gospel-writers all agree that three days later Jesus was brought back to life by the power of God. These two events, the death and resurrection of Jesus, were at the heart of the preaching of the early Christian Church and have stood at the very centre of the Christian faith ever since.

In recent years we have learned much more about the world into which Jesus of Nazareth was born. We know that his life and teaching were deeply affected by the political, religious and social environment in which he spent nearly all of his life. Many of his parables (stories carrying a spiritual meaning), for instance, took their inspiration from everyday life in Palestine, and his social teaching often sprang from the needs and concerns of those around him – on topics ranging widely from family life, marriage and divorce to paying taxes to the Romans and taking oaths.

Two great forces, one political and the other religious, clashed bitterly during the time of Jesus: the Roman empire with all its brutality and authoritarianism and the Jewish religion with its strong traditions and dependence on divine revelation. It is important to know something of both

Jerusalem, from the Mount of Olives towards the old city. The Dome of the Rock marks the site of Herod's Temple.

these forces to understand many of the events and much of the teaching found in the Gospels. By the time Jesus was born the Romans had been established in Palestine for five decades and the people despaired of any visible hope of future salvation. The Roman occupation aroused violently strong emotions. Meanwhile, the Jewish faith, 2,000 years old, stood as a great bulwark in the way of Jesus and his message.

A certain Galilean, whose name was Judas, prevailed with his countrymen to revolt; and said they were cowards if they would endure to pay a tax to the Romans, and would, after God, submit to mortal men as their lords.

FLAVIUS JOSEPHUS (37–c. 95 CE),
JEWISH HISTORIAN

THE WORLD OF JESUS

Contents

The Land of Palestine

Although Palestine was a tiny country it has had an enormous influence on religious history, including that of Christianity.

The Jewish homeland, Palestine, was very small, measuring no more than 230 kilometres long and 80 kilometres at its widest point. It was located between the Mediterranean Sea and the desert, at the meeting-point of three continents – Europe, Asia and Africa. This made Palestine commercially and strategically important, and from earliest times it acted as a land bridge across which merchants and armies freely travelled.

The most important geographical features of Palestine were the coastal plain, the plain of Esdraelon, the central uplands, the wilderness of Judea and the River Jordan:

The coastal plain
The coastal plain was a narrow strip of land that stretched for

over 160 kilometres from Tyre and Sidon in the north to the plain of Philistia in the south.

The strip was only five kilometres wide in the north but 40 kilometres across in the south. Mount Carmel split the coastal plain into two. Jesus spent some time in the north, where he met a Syro-Phoenician woman and healed her daughter.

The plain of Esdraelon
This area, to the east of Mount Carmel, saw many battles in the Old Testament period. Jesus visited Nain to restore a widow's son to life.

The central uplands
The central uplands are a range of mountains in the north of Galilee, almost 1,200 metres high. It was there, in Nazareth, that Jesus was raised and spent most of his life. Down towards Jerusalem, a city which stood on four hills, the land became more barren. Jesus probably paid several visits to Jerusalem, a place holy to all the Jews, before spending the last days of his life in the city.

The wilderness of Judea

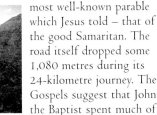

The road from Jerusalem to Jericho was the setting for the most well-known parable which Jesus told – that of the good Samaritan. The road itself dropped some 1,080 metres during its 24-kilometre journey. The Gospels suggest that John the Baptist spent much of his time in this wilderness area and that the temptations of Jesus also took place there.

The Jordan valley

The River Jordan journeys to the Dead Sea via the Sea of Galilee, a sizeable freshwater lake. It was on the western shore of this lake that Jesus found his first disciples, who were fishermen, and spent the early days of his ministry. Below the Sea of Galilee the Jordan descended still further to the Dead Sea, which was 360 metres below sea-level and the lowest inhabited point on the earth's surface.

The Sea of Galilee is given several different names in the Gospels. Apart from the Sea of Galilee it is also called the sea or lake of Tiberias, Chinnereth ('harp-shaped') and Gennesaret.

Galilee

Jesus spent most of his life and the years of his public ministry in lowland Galilee. Most of his best-known parables took their inspiration from the area and many of his miracles were also performed there.

In the time of Jesus Galilee was the most northerly region in Palestine. It was a densely populated area with many towns and villages – 204 according to Josephus, the Jewish historian, who was also Roman governor of the area. Most people lived in rural areas and worked the land. Although the land was rich and the Sea of Galilee provided a plentiful supply of fish, the area was known for its poverty. The people living there were dismissed by their contemporaries as poor and ignorant peasants.

The Sea of Galilee

Apart from agriculture, fishing on the Sea of Galilee was the main source of employment in Galilee. This lake was below sea-level and surrounded by very high hills – a combination which produced the sudden squalls and storms which are mentioned several times in the Gospels. It was the scene of two of the 'nature' miracles of Jesus – the stilling of the storm and the walking of Jesus on the water. Jesus also found four of his disciples – James, John, Andrew and Peter – who were fishermen on the shore of the

The Sea of Galilee and the villages on its shores supplied the backdrop for much of Jesus' Galilean ministry.

Then Jesus began to denounce the cities in which most of his miracles had been performed, because they did not repent. 'Woe to you, Korazin! Woe to you, Bethsaida! If the miracles that were performed in you had been performed in Tyre and Sidon, they would have repented long ago in sackcloth and ashes.'

MATTHEW 11:20–21

Capernaum and performed more miracles in the area than anywhere else. A ruined synagogue dating from the fourth or fifth century CE has been discovered in Capernaum and this may have been built on the site of one which dates back to the first century – presumably the one in which Jesus preached.

Sea of Galilee before he called them to follow him. It appears that Jesus often used the hills around the lake as a quiet place in which to pray.

Galilee and Jesus

Jesus grew up in the town of Nazareth, but he moved to Capernaum on the northern shore of the Sea of Galilee to begin his public ministry. He frequently spent time there, probably living in the house of Peter. Jesus probably preached more sermons in the synagogue in

Korazin, a town on the shore of the Sea of Galilee condemned by Jesus. Even the miracles he performed there failed to bring the people to repentance.

The fifth-century synagogue at Capernaum probably stands on the site of the one in which Jesus preached.

The rural nature of the area clearly had a great influence on the teaching of Jesus, since most of his parables have an agricultural setting. The parables of the sower and the lost sheep, for instance, sit very comfortably in a Galilean context. At the same time two towns in Galilee, Korazin and Bethsaida, exasperated Jesus because they failed to respond to the miracles he performed there. Jesus cursed them, comparing them to the notoriously wicked towns of Tyre and Sidon.

Life Under the Romans

For centuries before the birth of Jesus the land of Palestine had been under foreign control – first the Greeks and then the Romans. The Romans appointed Herod the Great to rule Palestine and allowed the Jews a small measure of self-rule in religious matters.

When Jesus was born it had been a long time since Palestine had enjoyed the luxury of running its own affairs without outside interference. Between 333 BCE and the Roman invasion in 63 BCE many Greek customs had been introduced into the country (a process known as 'Hellenization'), and among the many innovations was the use of the Greek language. Judas Maccabeus, a charismatic figure thought by some to be the Jewish Messiah, led a revolt in the second century against this Greek influence.

Caesar Augustus reigned at the time of Jesus' birth. Herod had been appointed king of Judea by Mark Antony, but after Augustus defeated Antony, Herod quickly switched his loyalty.

the country on their behalf and he continued to do so until his death in 4 BCE. By all contemporary accounts Herod was a ruthless but shrewd ruler, who was willing to eliminate anyone he believed to be disloyal or a threat to his throne. Among others he killed his favourite wife, his mother-in-law, his brother-in-law, three sons and several close friends. Herod was the

Herod the Great

The Romans became involved in Palestinian affairs in 63 BCE when Pompey invaded the country. In 37 BCE Herod the Great, a half-Jew, was able to secure Roman support to govern

> *He [Judas Maccabeus] extended the glory of his people.*
> *Like a giant he put on his breastplate;*
> *he bound on his armour of war and waged battles,*
> *protecting the camp by his sword.*
> *He was like a lion in his deeds, like a lion's cub roaring for prey.*
> *He searched out and pursued those who broke the law.*
>
> APOCRYPHA, 1 MACCABEES 3:3–5

AFTER HEROD

When Herod died in 4 BCE the Romans took the opportunity to divide Palestine between his three sons. One of them, Archelaus, was so cruel that Jewish protests led to him being replaced by a Roman governor (procurator), a post to which Pontius Pilate was later appointed in 26 CE. Pilate stayed in the post for 10 years before being replaced by the Romans, again for using excessive cruelty.

Temple in Jerusalem, but the building project took so long it continued way beyond his death. Other building projects carried out under the king's instructions included temples to Roman gods as well as the rebuilding of Samaria, which was renamed Sebaste – the Greek term for the Latin *Augustus*. He also built a magnificent harbour and town on the Mediterranean coast which was named Caesarea, also in honour of the Roman emperor.

king of Judea when Jesus was born in Bethlehem in 5/4 BCE.

Herod tried to please the Jews by building a magnificent

The ruined Israelite city of Samaria was rebuilt by Herod the Great and renamed Sebaste.

Everyday Life in Palestine

Traders and merchants passed through Palestine on their way to and from the Middle East and the Mediterranean Sea.

Jesus tended to avoid the key trade-routes through Palestine and instead travelled mainly on foot with his disciples across country and on minor roads. As the parable of the good Samaritan shows, such travelling could be lonely and very dangerous.

Coinage

Roman coinage was used throughout the empire, but there were several local forms of coinage in use as well. The denarius was the most widely used coin in Palestine and was used to pay taxes to the Romans: this coin bore the portrait of the emperor. Jesus commented on this when he was challenged about the paying of such taxes, since using Roman coins was a constant reminder to Jews that they were a subject people. There was also a special coinage for paying the Temple tax and it was the unscrupulous business of changing one to the other that Jesus objected to so strongly.

A denarius bearing the portrait of the Roman emperor. The coin was the the equivalent of a day's wage at the time of Jesus.

Work

Palestine was largely an agricultural country and there are many references to farming in the Gospels, especially in the parables that Jesus told. From the parable of the rich fool, it seems that farming could be a

Although a woman could own property in first-century Palestine, it was only as a mother that she gained the respect of society. Unmarried and childless women were socially ostracized. This scorn was only removed from the childless Elizabeth, the mother of John the Baptist, when by God's grace she became pregnant at an advanced age.

Jesus frequently used images from agriculture to illustrate his teaching. The struggle to make a living from the land continues today.

on a subsistence basis. Wheat was the staple diet of people in Palestine, although barley, olives and vines were also grown widely. Ploughing and sowing took place at the beginning of November after early rains, but unforeseen spells of drought were a constant danger. Farmers sowed seed by hand and this familiar sight was the basis for Jesus' famous parable of the sower. The crop was harvested in May or June.

Jesus chose some of his first disciples from among the fishermen of Capernaum, on the Sea of Galilee. The Gospels indicate that fishing was often done at night.

highly profitable occupation. At the same time it was clearly hard for those labourers at the bottom of the agricultural ladder.

Much of the farming was

MARRIAGE AND FAMILY LIFE

When a couple were betrothed, a written document was signed, followed by a marriage ceremony after which the bride was taken into the groom's home. Divorce was relatively easy to obtain, although it was officially discouraged by the religious authorities.

Children were expected to submit to their parents' authority at all times, while the father carried the responsibility of providing for all the members of his family.

Fishing

Fishing was very important to the Palestinian economy and could be very profitable. The first disciples of Jesus were fishermen and Jesus made much use of the symbolism of their profession. For example, Jesus promised Peter and his brother Andrew that instead of catching fish they would catch men for the kingdom of God.

17

Jewish Religious Institutions

Jewish religious life in first-century Palestine was built on three institutions: the Temple in Jerusalem, the synagogues dotted around the country and the Sanhedrin, the religious council sanctioned by the Romans.

According to Jewish sources the Sanhedrin met in the Chamber of Hewn Stone in the Temple. They appointed up to 23 members to function in larger towns and cities, and as few as seven elders in smaller towns.

The most important religious institution for the Jewish people was the Temple in Jerusalem.

The Temple

The whole Temple complex covered about 143,800 square metres, with the outer court, named the Court of the Gentiles, open to everyone. Only Jewish people, though, could enter the Court of the Women where most acts of worship, apart from sacrifices, took place. Only men could enter the Court of the Israelites. Priests alone could enter the Holy Place and only the High Priest, on the Day of Atonement each year, could enter directly into God's presence in the Holy of Holies.

The primary element in Jewish worship at the time was animal sacrifice and this could only take place within the Temple precincts. Apart from coming to the Temple to offer their sacrifices, Jewish people also came to present tithes and offerings, fulfil religious vows, and pray, worship and receive cleansing after ritual defilement. In the outer courts of the Temple teaching and discussion about the Jewish law took place, as well as the buying and selling of animals for sacrifice and the exchanging of foreign currency for Jewish coins to use for the Temple offerings.

The Law forbade representations of people or animals in religious art. These carvings from the synagogue at Capernaum are of pomegranates.

The synagogue

For Jews outside Jerusalem the synagogue, rather than the Temple, was the most familiar religious institution. In the time of Jesus most of the synagogues were private homes in which Jews came together to pray and study. While worship in the Temple was dominated by priests, in a synagogue it was conducted by members of the congregation who took

on different leadership roles. Services largely comprised readings from the scriptures, a sermon and prayers and were held on the Sabbath day and during the week. Distinguished visitors, such as Jesus on occasions, would be invited to give the sermon.

The Sanhedrin

The Sanhedrin was the main judicial and leglislative body within Judaism. It was responsible for interpreting the law, making new laws, conducting trials and imposing punishments for the Jewish community. The Sanhedrin was a council made up of 70 members, mainly priests and scribes, plus the High Priest who acted as its leader. The Sadducees were a small group with a great influence on the Jewish religion because the High Priest and many of the members of the Sanhedrin were drawn from its membership.

A model of the Temple complex in Jesus' time. The tallest building was the Holy Place, within which was the Holy of Holies. Surrounding it was the Court of the Israelites, open only to Jewish men. The adjoining courtyard was the Court of the Women, and the large area enclosed by the colonnaded walkway was open to Gentiles.

Jewish Beliefs

First-century Judaism was a proudly monotheistic faith which placed great emphasis upon the importance of the Torah and the hope that God would send the Messiah to deliver his people.

Jews in first-century Palestine were surrounded by many other faiths, but the one thing that always distinguished them from all others was a strict monotheism – belief in one God – while the religious world around them was invariably polytheistic – believing in many deities. From its birth some 2,000 years earlier, Judaism had strongly maintained the uniqueness and sovereignty of God. The *Shema* is the classic expression of this faith in the one God – a faith which was shared by Jesus and most of his early followers, since they too were Jews.

The scriptures

The Jewish scriptures, the foundation of the faith, were made up of the Torah (Law), the Nevi'im (Prophets) and the Ketuvim (Writings). The most important part of the scriptures was the Torah, the first five books of the Bible. This tells the story of the creation of the world, the release of the Jews from slavery (the Exodus), the giving of the law to Moses and the entry of the Jews into the Promised Land of Canaan.

The Messiah

The Messiah, the 'anointed one', was originally a person set apart by God for a special task. The title normally referred to kings, but it was also used in the scriptures to refer to priests and prophets. It came to mean a future deliverer, a descendant of King David, who would deliver Israel from its enemies, accomplish God's purposes, and set up the divine kingdom on earth. Christians came to see Jesus as the Messiah but the Jews did not share this belief.

A first-century phylactery and the tiny parcels of thin skin which it contained. The leather phylactery was strapped to its owner's head, and the skin was covered with verses from the Old Testament in minute writing. All are shown actual size.

Torah scrolls are treated with great respect, and are housed in the wall of the synagogue in a specially constructed cupboard known as the ark.

Hear, O Israel: the Lord our God, the Lord is one. Love the Lord your God with all your heart and with all your soul and with all your strength. These commandments that I give you today are to be upon your hearts. Impress them on your children. Talk about them when you sit at home and when you walk along the road, when you lie down and when you get up.

THE *SHEMA*, DEUTERONOMY 6:4–7

Worship

The Temple and the synagogues were at the centre of Jewish worship. Sacrifices were at the heart of Temple worship, but common people only offered them on rare occasions. It was in the synagogues in towns and villages that people met for study, prayer, sermons and the reading of the scriptures.

Devout Jews were expected to pray twice a day at home, in the morning and the afternoon, at times which corresponded to the daily sacrifices in the Temple. The *Shema* was said twice daily in the morning and evening, with blessings said before and after every meal. The people attached fringes or tassels to the corners of their garments; placed a mezuzah (a leather box containing the *Shema*) on the doorpost of each room in the house and wore tefillin (black leather boxes containing verses from scripture) when praying – all of which were special symbols of their faithfulness to God and his laws.

Jewish Festivals

Festivals played a significant part in Jewish religious life and none more so than Passover. The Sabbath day, a weekly festival, had a considerable effect on the everyday lives of Jewish people.

The most important day of the week for Jews was the Sabbath day, the seventh day of the week. No work was allowed on the Sabbath day, a day which was marked by synagogue worship and special family meals. Although the Jewish scriptures gave no guidance about what could and could not be done on the Sabbath day, a large amount of oral tradition was available to guide all believers in their behaviour. For Jews dispersed throughout the Roman empire keeping the Sabbath day was a distinctive practice that set them apart from other people and religions. Some of the fiercest disagreements that Jesus had with the Jewish religious leaders were over keeping the Sabbath day.

The Passover

By the time of Jesus, worship was largely centred on the local synagogue, although the major festivals of the Passover, Sukkot and Shavuot drew thousands of pilgrims to the Temple in Jerusalem. The Passover reminded Jews of the time in their national history when their ancestors were rescued by God from slavery in Egypt. There were two parts to its celebration:

◆ The ritual slaughter of paschal (Passover) lambs in the Temple, lambs which were supplied by the worshippers themselves.
◆ The eating of the lambs in a family meal which had to be held within the city limits.

The Gospels only refer to the second part of this celebration

> *All the men of your nation are to come to worship the Lord three times a year at the one place of worship: at Passover, Harvest Festival [Shavuot], and the Festival of Shelters [Sukkot]. Each man is to bring a gift as he is able, in proportion to the blessings that the Lord your God has given him.*
>
> DEUTERONOMY 16:16–17

and this is clearly the meal that Jesus enjoyed with his disciples on the eve of his arrest by the Roman authorities. The fact that Jesus celebrated it with his disciples shows that he had come to regard them as his 'family'.

Crowds gather at the Western Wall in Jerusalem for a bar mitzvah celebration.

OTHER FESTIVALS

Apart from Passover John's Gospel mentions three other festivals for which Jesus travelled to Jerusalem. The first is simply described as 'the festival of the Jews', which may have been Pentecost or the Jewish New Year. This was the time when Jesus healed the disabled man by the pool of Bethesda. The second is the Feast of Tabernacles, during which water was ritually drawn from the local well and the Temple lit up with candles. It was on this occasion that Jesus appropriately referred to himself as the light of the world and the water of life. The third is the less important festival of Hanukkah, which celebrated the rededication of the Temple in 164 BCE by Judas Maccabeus after it had been profaned by King Antiochus Epiphanes. Jesus spoke of himself as the one dedicated to God who would replace the Temple in the plan of God.

Jewish Religious Groups

The two main Jewish groups mentioned in the Gospels for their opposition to Jesus are the Pharisees and the Sadducees. A third group, the Essenes, are not mentioned at all, while a fourth group, the Zealots, were violently opposed to the Roman presence in Palestine.

The Pharisees were the largest of the Jewish religious groups during the time of Jesus – they numbered about 6,000 in Jerusalem alone. They took their name and their attitude towards religious faith from the Hebrew verb meaning 'to separate'. They stressed all aspects of the law, the Torah, and accepted the divine origin of the Prophets and the Writings in their scriptures. They imposed many additional laws on the people to safeguard the purity of the Torah. They believed strongly in the immortality of the soul, the resurrection of the body and the existence of angels. The Pharisees are the group most frequently mentioned in the Gospels for their vehement opposition to Jesus.

> For there are three philosophical sects among the Jews. The followers of the first of whom are the Pharisees; of the second the Sadducees; and the third sect, who pretends to a severer discipline, are called Essenes... the doctrine of the Sadducees is this: That souls die with the bodies; nor do they regard the observation of anything besides what the law enjoins them.
>
> FLAVIUS JOSEPHUS (37–c. 95 CE), JEWISH HISTORIAN

The Sadducees

The Sadducees were a small but highly influential group of aristocratic landowners from whose number the High Priest was always chosen. This, together with their extensive representation in the Sanhedrin, was the source of their influence. In order to maintain this influence they were prepared to compromise with the Roman authorities. Both the Jewish historian Josephus and the New Testament record that the Sadducees rejected belief in the resurrection of the dead, with the Gospels adding that they did not believe in angels or spirits either. Their largely materialistic view of religious faith emphasized the importance of Temple ritual.

The Essenes

Although the Essenes are not mentioned in the New Testament many people think that John the Baptist may have spent some time in an Essene community before becoming a highly controversial public figure. If so, the community to which he belonged was

THE ZEALOTS

The Zealots were a right-wing, nationalistic group in first-century Palestine ready to use force to expel the Romans from their home country. They were closely allied with another group, the Sicarii, who took their name from *sica*, the dagger which they carried with them to plunge into any Roman soldier if opportunity arose.

Ritual bath house of the Essene community at Qumran on the edge of the Dead Sea.

probably that at Qumran, on the shore of the Dead Sea. It is this community which buried numerous scrolls in clay pots as the Roman army advanced on them in 68 CE. These scrolls were unearthed by a Bedouin goatherd in 1947. These Dead Sea Scrolls, as they are called, provided us with one of the most exciting biblical archaeological finds of all time.

Although the New Testament begins with the four Gospels of Matthew, Mark, Luke and John, these are not the earliest books in the New Testament to have been written. The many letters, or epistles, of Paul were composed before the first Gospel (almost certainly Mark's) was written. Paul wrote the earliest of his letters around 49 CE and was probably put to death by the Roman emperor, Nero, sometime between 64 and 66 CE. Mark wrote his Gospel about the same time as Paul was killed, with the other three Gospels following sometime afterwards.

It is not certain that any of the four Gospels were written by eyewitnesses to the events they describe and, with the possible exception of Luke, the identity of their authors is far from clear. The Gospels stand at the end of a chain of tradition in which the teachings and

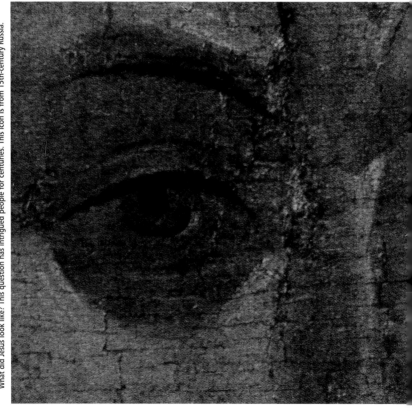

What did Jesus look like? This question has intrigued people for centuries. This icon is from 15th-century Russia.

stories of Jesus were transmitted and preserved in written and oral form for more than 30 years after the death of Jesus, before they were cast in anything approaching the form that we have today.

A Gospel is a narrative, fashioned out of selected traditions, that focuses on the activity and speech of Jesus as a way to reveal his character and develops a dramatic plot that culminates in the stories of his passion and resurrection.

J.L. BAILEY AND L.D. VAN DER BROEK

KNOWING ABOUT JESUS

Contents

Oral Traditions and Written Records

For many years after the death of Jesus information about his life and teaching was kept alive by word of mouth. It was some time before anything was written down and decades before the first Gospel was produced.

Jesus did not leave any written record of his teaching. He was a travelling preacher and teacher whose words lodged in the hearts and minds of his listeners to be long remembered. Written records of his words and deeds only became available to succeeding generations because Jesus had followers who believed them to be important enough to record and pass down.

Oral traditions

The traditions about Jesus existed for a long time in a largely oral form. This was perfectly normal in a culture where oral communication was used in every area of life. Very few people in Palestine could read or write and the teachings of Jesus were largely given in the first place to illiterate peasants who kept them alive in the only way they knew – by passing them on verbally. We know nothing of the level of education enjoyed by Jesus, although a reference to him reading from the Jewish scriptures in public suggests that he was reasonably educated.

The techniques of passing down stories from one generation to the next, common in Bible times, are still alive in some places today. This storyteller in modern Iran relates the epic of Alexander the Great

I did not suppose that information from books could help me so much as the word of a living and surviving voice.

PAPIAS, SECOND-CENTURY
CHRISTIAN LEADER

The stories about Jesus and various collections of his teachings were passed on from one person to another and from one Christian community to another. These traditions were used by the early Christians in different ways. In preaching to those outside the Christian community they would have recounted the things that Jesus did, but in helping new converts to the faith his teachings would have been particularly highly valued. When controversies arose within the different Christian communities, as they often did, then an appropriate action or word of Jesus would have been recalled and used to settle any dispute.

Oral traditions are more fluid than written records. The retelling of the stories in different situations to meet a variety of needs led to them being shaped and reshaped by the storytellers over a period of time. This explains, for instance, why there are marked differences in the Gospels

WRITTEN RECORDS

By the sixth decade of the first century the need to preserve written accounts of the life and teaching of Jesus became paramount. The original apostles, the supreme depository of the truth about Jesus, were dying, as were many of the other eyewitnesses. Some of the information about Jesus was in danger of dying with them. Moreover, the Christian community was expanding throughout the Mediterranean world and many converts, with little background knowledge, were joining the Church. An effective means of teaching them some basic truths about Jesus was needed. Thus the four Gospels were written by the end of the first century.

between records of the same event. Although oral traditions changed over time, this nevertheless does not affect their basic historicity.

29

What is a Gospel?

The four Gospels in the New Testament are not straightforward descriptions of the life of Jesus; rather, they are the selective accounts of four evangelists, whose concern it is to present the truth of the Christian gospel as they see it for the audience they want to reach.

The four Gospels in the New Testament are not 'biographies' of Jesus in the modern sense of that word. Only two of them – Matthew and Luke – give us any information at all about his birth, while the only other recorded event from the first 30 years of his life took place when he was 12 years old – and that is included by only one Gospel! The remainder of the four Gospels is concerned with, at most, a bare three years of adult life, with some 25 per cent of the material in all four Gospels being taken up with the last few days in Jesus' life.

The nature of the Gospels

The Gospel-writers concentrate on certain events in the life of Jesus because these were of particular interest to them. They were writing as Christian believers; as one modern commentator puts it, 'they saw Jesus with the eyes of faith'. This does not mean they are unreliable witnesses, but simply that they are selective in their choice of material, using their sources to support their own purposes in writing. Each Gospel-writer also has his own target audience in mind and his choice of material reflects this.

The opening sentence of Mark's Gospel gives us a clue about the nature of this Gospel and all the others.

History in the Gospels is history seen by Christians. A non-Christian would see it differently – claiming, for instance, that the resurrection could not have happened. It might be interesting to have an account of Jesus written from that point of view, but none has come down to us. What we have are the Gospels, written by Christian believers, written to persuade people to believe, but none the less historical for that.

I. HOWARD MARSHALL

The scribes who made copies of the Gospels during the Middle Ages turned them into wonderful works of art. This title page from the *Book of Kells* shows symbols of the four evangelists and was produced in an Irish monastery.

life-transforming. He was also concerned with the worldwide spread of the Christian message and in this sense could truly be described as an 'evangelist'.

This is clearly the task that Luke sets himself. In the preamble to his Gospel he explains that his overall purpose is to help people know the truth personally of the very things about Jesus that they had already been taught. Luke goes further than the other Gospel-writers: in the Acts of the Apostles he provides the only history that we have of the early Christian Church. Acts describes the growth and personalities of the Church in the years following the Day of Pentecost. Its purpose is to highlight the continuity between the life of Jesus and that of the Christian community, an essential element of the apostolic message.

Mark describes his work as 'the beginning of the gospel of Jesus Christ'. It is clear that each writer had accepted the authority of Christ over his own life and was writing as a committed member of the Christian community in order to interest and convert others. He was deeply involved in the task of spreading the Christian message – not just teaching the bare facts of Christian belief but showing how that message could be

Mark's Gospel

Three of the four Gospels in the New Testament have a lot of material in common and take a similar approach to the life of Jesus. They are called the Synoptic ('looking together') Gospels.

The relationship between the four Gospels in the New Testament has been the subject of intense debate and speculation among biblical scholars for decades. It is now generally agreed that Mark was the first Gospel to be written, followed a decade or so afterwards by Matthew and Luke. John's Gospel is very different from the other three and followed towards the end of the first century. Surprisingly, for centuries Mark's Gospel was largely neglected by the Christian Church in its worship as it was considered to be little more than a summary of the other three Gospels.

Mark the author

It is important to remember that none of the Gospels actually identifies the person who wrote it, so we cannot be sure about the authorship of any of them. 'Mark' may well have been the 'John Mark' mentioned in the Acts of the Apostles, who was a travelling companion of Paul. If so, Mark's Gospel was probably written from Rome around 65 CE. This was about the time when the Church was undergoing its first persecution at the hands of the Roman emperor, Nero, a persecution

Mark became Peter's interpreter and wrote accurately all that he remembered, not indeed, in order, of the things said and done by the Lord. For he had not heard the Lord, nor had he followed him, but later on, as I said, followed Peter, who used to give teaching as necessity demanded but not making, as it were, an arrangement of the Lord's oracles, so that Mark did nothing wrong in thus writing down single points as he remembered them.

PAPIAS, SECOND-CENTURY
CHRISTIAN LEADER

Mark writing his Gospel. The lunette above this shows the baptism of Christ.
From *Codex Ebnerianus*, Byzantine, early 12th century.

the Messiah was expected to show when he appeared: he forgave the sins of the people, was able to calm the unruly elements of nature and frequently healed the sick.

At the same time, in a Gospel that moves along at a breathless pace, Jesus was open to the full range of human emotions. He displayed real anger, was easily moved by the suffering that he saw and found it very difficult to come to terms with his own impending death. Mark's Jesus was a decisive figure, a man in a hurry, busy breaking down the apparent barriers between heaven and earth through his healing ministry and his saving death. In the course of this public life, which may have lasted for little more than a year, he had many encounters with Satan in the form of demon-possession, sickness and a natural order capable of exacting great, and frightening, vengeance.

which had already claimed the lives of Peter and Paul. If this is the case then the author of the very first Gospel was certainly not a prominent member of the early Christian community.

Mark's portrait of Jesus

Mark begins and ends his Gospel with a clear statement of the divinity of Jesus, but in between suggests that anyone hinting at the divinity or the Messiahship of Jesus was told to keep quiet about it. This 'Messianic secret' has fascinated scholars for a long time. Why was Jesus so reluctant for others to openly acknowledge him as the Messiah? Mark's Jesus had all the hallmarks that

Matthew's and Luke's Gospels

Both Matthew and Luke in their Gospels leave us with much fuller and more considered accounts of the life and teaching of Jesus.

There are problems associated with the traditional ascription of Matthew's Gospel to Matthew, the tax-collecting disciple of Jesus. We cannot be certain when it was written either, although most scholars suggest a date sometime between 80 and 100 CE. The nature of Matthew's Gospel is much easier to assess.

Matthew's Gospel

Matthew's Gospel is the most noticeably Jewish of the four Gospels, perhaps because the author wrote for a largely Jewish audience. He was probably a Jewish-Christian scribe whose overriding concern was to present Jesus as the teaching Messiah, the fulfilment of all Jewish expectations. He certainly set out to show how many apects of Jesus life were foretold in the Jewish scriptures; 'it is written' is a favourite phrase of the author.

Matthew's Gospel contains the largest collection of Jesus' sayings found anywhere in the New Testament, and the Sermon on the Mount is at its heart. Matthew also has more to say than anyone else about the kingdom of God (or the kingdom of heaven as he often calls it). Scholars agree that this concept was central to Jesus' teaching.

Luke's Gospel

Tradition ascribes the authorship of Luke's Gospel to a doctor and travelling companion of Paul

A portrait of the evangelist Matthew. The lunette above this shows the nativity. From *Codex Ebnerianus*, Byzantine, early 12th century.

Heaven and earth will pass away,
but my words will never pass away.

MATTHEW 24:35

called the 'beloved physician'. Written around the same time as Matthew's Gospel, Luke's work is the first of two volumes (Acts is the second) dedicated to a high-ranking Roman official, Theophilus, about whom we know nothing.

Luke begins and ends his Gospel in the city of Jerusalem, emphasizing the importance of the sermon preached by Jesus in the synagogue at Nazareth. This sermon included most of the major themes of Luke's Gospel: the Holy Spirit, the healing of the poor and oppressed, the importance of preaching and God's activity outside the nation of Israel among the Gentiles. The Holy Spirit plays a particularly prominent role in this Gospel, as you would expect from the author of the Acts of the Apostles.

The author is also interested in those people on the very margins of Jewish society – women, children, outcasts and those who were disabled. For a doctor this interest is hardly surprising and Luke describes them as being 'blessed'. There is also an emphasis on prayer in the Gospel, so that Luke alone among the Gospel-writers includes the extended prayers of Zechariah, Simeon and Mary in his opening chapters and several references to Jesus praying at crucial times in his life.

Luke working on his account of the life of Jesus. The lunette above this shows the annunciation. From *Codex Ebnerianus*, Byzantine, early 12th century.

The Synoptic Problem

The so-called 'Synoptic problem' refers to the similarities and differences between the first three Gospels in the New Testament – the Synoptic Gospels. How did these similarities and differences arise and why are all three Gospels so different from the fourth Gospel?

The Synoptic problem can be set out in the following way:

◆ If we assume that Mark's was the first Gospel to be written, Matthew and Luke clearly made use of it when writing their Gospels. This would explain why so much material is common to all three Gospels.

◆ Matthew and Luke share about 200 verses, largely sayings of Jesus, which are not found in Mark. Most scholars think that they had access to a document that Mark did not use and which is now lost. They call this document Q, from the German word *Quelle* meaning 'source'. This document seems to have been largely a collection of sayings with some narrative included, although it is possible that Q might have been in oral rather than written form.

◆ There is much material in Matthew's Gospel which is not found in either Mark or Luke. Some 250 verses are unique to Matthew's Gospel and this seems to come from Matthew's own source – called 'M'.

◆ Luke includes material which makes up around 50 per cent of his Gospel and is not

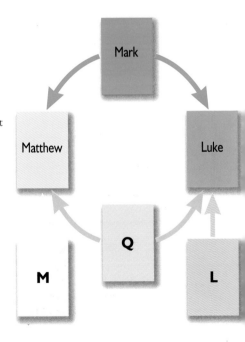

The relationship between the three Synoptic Gospels and their source material.

*Either the gospel is in all respects
identical with its earliest form
(in which case it came with its
time and has departed with it);
or else it contains something
which, under differing historical
forms, is of permanent validity.
The latter is the true view.*

ADOLPH VON HARNACK
(1851–1930), GERMAN CHURCH
HISTORIAN AND THEOLOGIAN

There are 661
verses in Mark's
Gospel, 1,068 in
Matthew's Gospel
(of which 606 are
taken from Mark)
and 1,149 verses
in Luke's Gospel
(of which 320 are
found in Mark).

Gospel on the different oral traditions circulating in the Christian Church at the time and, perhaps, some of the recollections of the apostle Peter.

Although four Gospels have survived there were clearly many others circulating. Luke opened his Gospel with an acknowledgment of this: 'Many have undertaken to draw up an account of the things that have been fulfilled among us.' Even John, who wrote many decades after the death of Jesus, openly admitted that he knew of many acts of Jesus that he left out of his own account.

found in either Matthew or Mark. This includes the stories of the birth of Jesus and many parables. This material is thought to come from 'L – Luke's own special source.

An explanation

Any answer put forward to solve the Synoptic problem must decide whether Mark's Gospel or Matthew's Gospel was written first. If, as most scholars believe, Mark's Gospel came first, it is simplest to assume that each evangelist used the documents and oral traditions that were available to him. Matthew used Mark's Gospel, the hypothetical 'Q' and his own source 'M'. Luke used Mark's Gospel, 'Q' and his own source 'L'. Mark, meanwhile, largely based his

John's Gospel

John's Gospel is very different from the other Gospels.
It presents far more of the extended discourses of Jesus
with far fewer of his miracles and none of his parables.

Although John's Gospel
covers some of the same
ground as the other Gospels it
does so in a strikingly
different way. An
early Church leader,
Clement of Alexandria,
described John's work
as a 'spiritual' Gospel
and there is much
truth in this.

Traditionally the
author of John's
Gospel has been
identified with the
'beloved disciple', a
member of the inner group of
disciples along with James and
Peter, but this is not certain.
It seems clear, though, that

this Gospel was the last of the
four to be written, towards the
end of the first century.

John uses the picture of
a lamp giving light to
illustrate the impact of Jesus
on a world in darkness.

Characteristics
John's Gospel opens
with the unique
identification of Jesus
with the divine *logos*
('word'), a concept
which combines the
Jewish idea of God's
self-expression with
the Greek concept of
the 'reason' behind the
universe. Jesus is the
divine Word,
spoken by

John dictating
his Gospel to
Prochros. The
lunette above
this shows
the harrowing
of hell.
From *Codex
Ebnerianus*,
Byzantine, early
12th century.

> *In the beginning was the Word, and
> the Word was with God, and the
> Word was God. He was with God
> in the beginning… The Word
> became flesh and lived for a while
> among us. We have seen his glory…
> No one has ever seen God, but
> God the only [Son], who is at the
> Father's side, has made him known.*
>
> JOHN 1:1–2, 14, 18

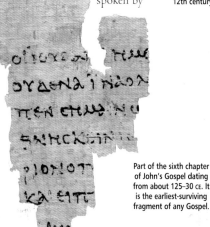

Part of the sixth chapter
of John's Gospel dating
from about 125–30 CE. It
is the earliest-surviving
fragment of any Gospel.

The 'I am' sayings

John alone records the seven sayings of Jesus which begin with the words 'I am': the bread of life; the light of the world; the sheep-gate; the good shepherd; the resurrection and the life; the way, truth and life; and the true vine. Most of these are traditional Jewish metaphors, used here to present Jesus as the reality to which each image points. There is no trace of them in any of the other Gospels, which shows that John probably had access to sources which the others did not have.

God, who came into the world as a human being. Just as Matthew and Luke start their Gospels with the incarnation of Jesus so does John, albeit along very different lines.

One of the great themes of John's Gospel is love: Jesus is the perfect gift of love, given by God to save the world and to convey God's promise of eternal life to everyone who believes. John paints a powerful picture of Jesus as the unquenchable light, shining in the darkness, who offers the gift of light to all those who are walking in darkness.

There are seven miracles of Jesus in John's Gospel and these are 'signs' so that the people could believe in him as their Messiah; these include the changing of water into wine at a wedding feast and the feeding of a large crowd. Throughout, the Gospel shows how Jesus fulfilled and yet transcended the Jewish scriptures. While the Gospel-writer believed that salvation came from the Jews he also records Jesus' severe condemnations of the Jewish leaders, which he delivered with great feeling.

Jesus Outside the Gospels

There are some references to Jesus outside the Gospels from early pagan and Jewish sources. These are sufficient to substantiate the existence of Jesus, but they do not add materially to our information about him.

Apart from the witness of the four canonical Gospels (Matthew, Mark, Luke and John – the Gospels accepted as authoritative and included in the New Testament) and a few other early Christian writers there is some clear evidence for Jesus' appearance in first-century Palestine from four non-Christian sources.

Tacitus

The Roman historian Tacitus governed Asia during the reign of Emperor Trajan (98–117 CE). Writing in the second century he referred to an infamous event involving Emperor Nero (54–68 CE) in 64 CE. Writing in his *Annals* Tacitus commented that the emperor had blamed a great fire which had decimated the city of Rome on 'a class hated for their abominations, who are commonly called Christians', although the emperor himself was widely thought to have been responsible. Tacitus went on to say that 'Chrestus', from whom the Christians took their name, was executed by the Roman procurator, Pontius Pilate, in the reign of Emperor Tiberius (14–37 CE)

The Roman Emperor Nero sparked off the Church's first wave of persecution when he blamed Christians for starting a fire that destroyed a large part of Rome.

Pliny

Pliny was the governor of Bithynia when he wrote to ask Emperor Trajan how he should deal with the Christians in his province. He informed the emperor that he gave any Christian arrested and brought before him three chances to recant. He discharged anyone who was prepared to deny that they were a Christian because by so doing 'they cursed Christ, a thing which, it is said, genuine Christians cannot be induced to do'.

Suetonius

Suetonius was secretary to Emperor Hadrian and wrote the biographies of 12 emperors. In his life of Claudius he refers to the fact that Claudius expelled all Christians from Rome 'since the Jews were continually making disturbances at the instigation of Chrestus'.

Josephus

Josephus was a Jewish historian who, after his capture by the Romans, was given a place in the Roman court. Writing about 94 CE he appears at first sight to be a more useful witness to Jesus than the other sources outside the Gospels, although there is some evidence to suggest that his writings were later tampered with by someone who was favourably disposed to the Christian cause. If this is not the case, then his witness to Jesus and the main events in his life is remarkably similar to that of the Gospels. In his *Jewish Antiquities* Josephus identifies Jesus as the brother of James and as the one who was called the Messiah.

The influence of Josephus was considerable: while later Jewish rabbinic texts do refer

The Jewish historian Josephus, whose summary of the life of Jesus is similar to that recorded in the four Gospels.

At this time there was a wise man who was called Jesus. And his conduct was good and he was known to be virtuous. And many people from among the Jews and from the other nations became his disciples. Pilate condemned him to be crucified and to die. And those who had become his disciples did not abandon his discipleship. They reported that he had appeared to them three days after his crucifixion and that he was alive. Accordingly he was perhaps the Messiah of whom the prophets have recounted wonders.

FLAVIUS JOSEPHUS (37–c. 95 CE), JEWISH HISTORIAN

to Jesus, they say little about him that is not found in Josephus – that he was a wise man who had followers; that he was a teacher; that he performed 'startling deeds'; that he was crucified by Pontius Pilate; and that he continued to have many followers after his death.

Christians believe that the birth of Jesus was the birth of God himself. Yet this miracle has to be seen within the context of the Jewish faith. This is why Matthew and Luke trace the genealogy of Jesus back through many great figures in Jewish history.

The shepherds and the wise men responded to an angelic visitation telling them exactly where the baby, God's Son, was to be found. The birth of Jesus was unique, yet human, and even King Herod bore unsuspecting witness to this. On hearing that a new 'king' had been born, he slaughtered all the baby boys in Bethlehem, desperate to kill his potential rival. By this time, however, Mary and Joseph were taking

The Finding of the Saviour in the Temple by William Holman Hunt (1827–1910).

Jesus to safety in Egypt. God was already protecting his Son because he had a vital role for him to play.

Jesus first showed the distinctiveness that was to characterize his ministry when he was 12 years old, asking questions of the Jewish rabbis in the Temple. They were astonished at the wisdom of one so young.

The central miracle asserted by Christians is the incarnation. They say that God became Man. Every other miracle prepares for this, or exhibits this, or results from this.

C.S. LEWIS (1898–1963),
IRISH-BORN WRITER, ACADEMIC
AND CHRISTIAN APOLOGIST

BEGINNINGS

Contents

The Ancestry of Jesus

Both Matthew and Luke trace the ancestry of Jesus back to its earliest Jewish roots as the context for the story of his birth. They demonstrate that Jesus had family links with Abraham and David, both of whom were regarded with great reverence within the Jewish community.

There are two genealogies of Jesus in the Gospels, one in Matthew and the other in Luke. Neither is intended to provide the reader with a full family tree, since they cannot be fully harmonized with one another. Rather, they are intended to show that a direct link could be traced between Jesus and all the great figures in Jewish history, as Jews would expect of the promised Messiah.

Abraham was the father of the Jewish nation, and one of the most important figures in the genealogy of Jesus. This illustration for All Souls' Day portrays Abraham with souls in his lap. From the *Legendary of Dominican Nuns of Holy Cross* (German, after 1271), Regensburg.

Matthew's genealogy

Matthew's genealogy is based on three epochs – from Abraham (c. 2000 BCE) to Jesse, the father of King David (c. 1000 BCE); from David to the Jewish exile in Babylon (586 BCE); and from the end of the exile to Jesus 'who is called Christ'. The first two of these epochs last for 14 generations, while the third only extends to 13 generations, although Matthew claims to list 14.

Abraham and David are the two most important figures in Matthew's genealogy. Abraham was the father of the Jewish nation and David was considered by Jews to have been the perfect king and the ideal for the future Messiah to emulate. The descent of Jesus from David shows that God's promise of a Messiah to the Jews had been fulfilled, through the royal line of Judah.

Luke's genealogy

Luke's genealogy does not follow the same scheme as Matthew's. Luke lists 42 generations between King David and Jesus, which would fit in neatly with the time span involved of about 1,000 years. While Matthew works forwards from Abraham, through David to Jesus, Luke's genealogy works backwards from Jesus.

Now Jesus himself was about 30 years old when he began his ministry. He was the son, so it was thought, of Joseph.

LUKE 3:23

Interestingly, Luke goes back further than Matthew by tracing the ancestry of Jesus beyond Abraham to Adam, 'the son of God'. This may simply reflect Luke's interest, apparent throughout his writing, in the universality of the gospel – it is a gospel that reaches beyond the Jews to all people. The phrase 'the Son of God' also reflects the acknowledgment by God that Jesus is his Son at his baptism in the River Jordan – an account of which immediately precedes the genealogy – and looks forward to the transfiguration of Jesus.

Some of the names that appear in Luke's genealogy, such as Levi, are priestly figures. This has led some to believe that Matthew traced the royal descent of Jesus, whereas Luke implied his priestly heritage. This would make Jesus the ideal Messiah – the perfect king and priest.

John the Baptist

Speculation was rife in early first-century Palestine that one of the old prophets would return to usher in the arrival of the Messiah. There were many who thought that John the Baptist was that figure.

Matthew and Mark tell us nothing about the early life of John the Baptist, but Luke interweaves the story of John's conception and birth with that of Jesus, his cousin. John's parents, Elizabeth and Zechariah, were well past normal child-bearing age when he was conceived. The births of both John and Jesus were miracles, although for very different reasons.

John in public

The time that John spent in the Judean wilderness at the beginning of his public life has prompted speculation that he may have been linked with the Essene monastic community at Qumran. He certainly shared with them a longing for the coming of the Messiah and a belief in personal purity through the ritual washing of the body. The washing that John offered the people was a once-and-for-all cleansing of the body and spirit through baptism, a cleansing offered to everyone who was willing to repent of their sins.

Jesus and John

Jesus was one of many drawn to the banks of the River Jordan while John was preaching and baptizing and it was after he had been baptized by John that Jesus began his public ministry. John's Gospel appears to suggest that Jesus and John initially worked together as members of the same religious renewal movement, but the other Gospel-writers are silent about this and it seems very unlikely.

Although John initially saw himself as preparing the path

A voice of one calling:
'In the desert prepare the
way for the Lord;
make straight in the wilderness
a highway for our God.
Every valley shall be raised up,
every mountain and hill made low;
the rough ground shall become level,
the rugged places a plain.
And the glory of the Lord
will be revealed,
and all humankind together
will see it.'

ISAIAH 40:3–5

John the Baptist announced the imminent coming of the Messiah. *Deesis Christ with St John the Baptist*, Hagia Sofia, Istanbul, Turkey.

for the coming of the Messiah who would baptize the people with the Holy Spirit rather than water, he later expressed doubts about the divine mission of Jesus. After being thrown into prison by Herod the Great's son (who had now succeeded his father), John sent some of his own followers to find out from Jesus whether he was God's chosen Messiah or not. 'Tell John how I heal the sick and preach good news to the poor,' Jesus told them. They would have understood the meaning of his words. Healing the sick and preaching good news to the poor was exactly the role that

the promised Messiah was expected to carry out.

Jesus had no doubt about the value of John's ministry, believing that John belonged to the old prophetic order, while at the same time acting as a bridge to a new way of understanding God. Jesus believed that John the Baptist was greater than all the prophets, but he also declared that the least in the kingdom of God was greater than John. John belonged to the old order, but Jesus had come to inaugurate the new.

47

The Annunciation

Many Christians, especially Roman Catholics and Eastern Orthodox believers, honour Mary, the mother of Jesus, as the supreme example of a human being who gives herself unreservedly to accept the will of God.

In first-century Palestine girls were often promised in marriage at a very early age, but there is no indication that Mary was very young when she was betrothed to Joseph (a direct descendant of King David) and conceived Jesus.

Matthew's Gospel describes the sudden appearance of 'an angel of the Lord' to Joseph, announcing the birth of Jesus, as the result of which he took Mary 'home as his wife'. Luke, though, describes the Angel Gabriel appearing to Mary and startling her with the words: 'Greetings, you who are highly favoured: the Lord is with you.' Gabriel goes on to tell Mary that she has been chosen by God to bear his Son, Jesus, who will reign over the house of Jacob and inherit the throne of King David, a kingdom that will never end.

THE MAGNIFICAT

Having received the news from the angel, Mary set off to visit Elizabeth, who was already six months pregnant despite her advanced age. Gabriel had told Mary that Elizabeth was living proof that nothing was impossible with God: if Elizabeth could become pregnant and give birth, so could Mary. Mary's song, the Magnificat, which followed her arrival in Elizabeth's house, is a song of triumph over adversity rejoicing in the way that God reverses the ordinary fortunes of people on earth, exalting those who occupy a lowly position. This is a theme taken up by Luke on more than one occasion in his Gospel. For centuries the Magnificat has been sung by Christians as part of their worship. Its message of help and encouragement for the poor has always inspired a Christian commitment to help those who are marginalized in society.

> *Mary's yes is a free, responsible yes by which she accepts being the vessel of the new creation to be embodied by her son Jesus. It is not the yes of self-denial, almost of irresponsibility, as it has been traditionally presented to us. Mary knows to whom she is committing herself.*
>
> ANA MARÍA BIDEGAIN, COLUMBIAN CATHOLIC CHURCH HISTORIAN

Mary is understandably confused by the news. How, she wonders, can she give birth to her special son when she is a virgin? The angel tells her that it is God, through the Holy Spirit, who will be the father of her child – a virgin birth. Confronted by such news Mary expresses her willingness to bear God's son – 'I am the Lord's servant… May it be to me as you have said.' Many Christians honour Mary because she is the perfect example of someone willing to obey God at whatever cost.

No woman has ever been the recipient of such a startling and an awe-inspiring message as the one that the angel delivered to Mary. *The Annunciation* by Duccio di Buoninsegna (c. 1255–c. 1318).

The Nativity

There are two accounts of the nativity (birth) of Jesus in the Gospels and they describe the event from very different points of view.

The story of the conception and birth of Jesus is found in two of the four Gospels, Matthew's and Luke's. Although they are very different they do have a common purpose: to show that God is working out his purposes through the lives of ordinary people.

Matthew's account

The account Matthew gives of the birth of Jesus is comparatively brief and lacking in colourful detail. It merely informs us that Jesus was born in Bethlehem, without supplying us with any extra information. The author inserts several quotations from the Jewish scriptures to show that the birth was long predicted and expected. He bases his description around Joseph, the child's father, since it is he who names the child, a very significant event in every Jewish family, while in Luke's Gospel it is Mary who is at the centre of the account. Matthew's narrative is almost entirely taken up with Joseph's worries about how he should handle the unforeseen situation.

King David was born in Bethlehem, and Micah prophesied that it would also be the birthplace of the promised Messiah.

BETHLEHEM AND NAZARETH

Both Matthew and Luke make it clear that Jesus was born in Bethlehem, a small town south of Jerusalem. Matthew implies that Bethlehem was the actual residence of Mary and Joseph, with the couple moving to Nazareth later. Luke, however, states that the couple lived in Nazareth but travelled to Bethlehem for a census shortly before Mary gave birth.

This child is destined to cause the falling and rising of many in Israel, and to be a sign that will be spoken against, so that the thoughts of many hearts will be revealed. And a sword will pierce your own soul too.

LUKE 2:34–35

Shepherds on the hills outside Bethlehem were startled by the appearance of an angel announcing the birth of one who would bring great joy to all people. They raced into the town to seek out the baby, who was lying in a manger. *The Adoration of the Shepherds* (c. 1630, Italian, Neapolitan).

Luke's account

Luke's account of the nativity is very different, revealing the strong poetic, narrative and theological talents that are also apparent elsewhere in his Gospel. One key feature of Luke's account is the interweaving of the conception and birth of John the Baptist with that of Jesus. Luke is keen to show that the two men were very close from the beginning, but he also stressed that Jesus was superior in every way. This superiority was that of the new way of Jesus over the old way of Judaism.

Mary rather than Joseph is at the heart of Luke's account. The Angel Gabriel appeared to her; she travelled to Elizabeth; she went through the ritual of purification after childbirth; and the holy man Simeon gave her a special prophecy about Jesus. Mary is presented as the perfectly obedient 'handmaiden of the Lord' who accepts that she is to give birth to God's Son, almost without question. Luke twice refers to Mary as keeping what had happened to her hidden in her heart, perhaps implying that he obtained this special information directly from the mother of Jesus herself.

The Virgin Birth

The two accounts of the birth of Jesus raise more than one awkward question, particularly concerning the virgin birth.

Both Matthew and Luke state clearly that Jesus was conceived in the womb of Mary by the Holy Spirit, without the involvement of any human father. This event is called the virgin birth although, more correctly, it should be called the 'virginal conception' of Jesus. The surprising thing is that this supernatural event is not mentioned anywhere else in the New Testament – not in the other two Gospels, or in the writings of Paul. There may be a simple explanation for this. The virginal conception may have been a family secret which Mary was only willing to share with the two Gospel-writers and no one else. It may not have been common knowledge until these two Gospels were published.

Mary's virginity

The tradition that Mary was a virgin when she conceived and gave birth to Jesus is a strong one. There is a problem, however. The Greek word which is usually translated 'virgin' in the New Testament means little more than 'young woman', one who has reached sexual maturity but not necessarily someone who has not had sexual intercourse.

To Matthew and Luke, however, the word clearly meant more than this. When the Angel Gabriel informed Mary that she was to become pregnant and give birth to God's Son her response was one of great surprise: 'How can this be, since I am a virgin?' The implication behind Mary's question is very clear: she has never had sexual intercourse, so how can she possibly be pregnant?

Luke made the situation

THE VIRGIN BIRTH IN THE NEW TESTAMENT

Neither Mark nor John shows any interest in the early life of Jesus. For reasons that are not immediately apparent Mark begins his Gospel with the ministry of John the Baptist, while John opens with an extended meditation on the meaning of the coming of Jesus. The absence of references to the virgin birth in the letters of Paul has to be seen in the wider context of his almost complete lack of interest in any details of the human life of Jesus.

even clearer. He simply described Mary as a 'virgin' who was betrothed to Joseph. The Jewish faith allowed a betrothal agreement to be broken if the woman was found not to be a virgin, since this automatically broke the arrangement on which the agreement had been made. Joseph clearly had this in mind when he thought that he might call everything off on learning that Mary was pregnant. The angel appeared to Joseph in a dream and reassured him that

Therefore the Lord himself will give you a sign: the virgin will be with child and will give birth to a son, and will call him Immanuel ['God with us'].

ISAIAH 7:14

no other man was the father of her child – the only father was the Holy Spirit.

The virgin birth of Jesus was a unique and mysterious fusion of the human and the divine. Icon of Mary and Jesus.

Early Visitors to Jesus

Matthew and Luke inform us that there were two groups of visitors who came to see the infant Jesus: the shepherds and the wise men. It was the symbolic importance of the two visits, rather than the visits in themselves, which were seen to be significant.

Local shepherds (in Luke's Gospel) and wise men from the East (in Matthew's Gospel) received a divine revelation encouraging them to visit the infant Jesus. We do not know exactly when these visits took place, although there is reason to think that some months elapsed after the birth before the wise men came to worship Jesus.

The shepherds

The visit of the shepherds, an idyllic story, underlines the interest that Luke shows elsewhere in his Gospel in the poorest members of society. It is typical of Luke that hordes of angels should announce the widespread rejoicing at the birth of Jesus and the ushering in of God's kingdom of peace to those languishing at the bottom of the social ladder. The shepherds were told that Jesus, the Messiah, had been born in David's birth city of Bethlehem.

Luke tells us that the shepherds were in the fields looking after their sheep when

The *Magi* brought gifts to Jesus, each of which symbolized some area of his life or ministry. *The Adoration of the Kings*, attributed to Zanobi Strozzi (1412–68).

the angels appeared – a common sight in Palestine, where sheep were turned out into the fields after June to feed on what remained of the harvest. This suggests that Jesus was born in the summer.

The angel said to them, 'Do not be afraid. I bring you good news of great joy that will be for all the people. Today in the town of David a Saviour has been born to you; he is Christ the Lord.'

LUKE 2:10–11

The use of the word 'Saviour' by the angels is striking. It is the only time that the word is used in the Synoptic Gospels.

The wise men

Matthew describes the visit of the wise men to see the infant Jesus after they had been guided by a star. Matthew calls the visitors *Magi*, which is probably best translated as 'magicians'. We do not know how many of them there were – just that they brought the three gifts of gold, frankincense and myrrh – nor do we have any independent corroboration of a star or comet appearing in the skies at this time.

By far the most important aspect of the visit of the wise men lies in its twofold symbolic significance and not in its historical details. The gold that the wise men brought symbolized the royal background of Jesus as the Son of man and Messiah; frankincense, used in Jewish religious rituals, pointed to the priestly ministry of Jesus; and

Shepherds were right at the bottom of the social hierachy, yet Jesus' birth was announced to them. An illumination by Maître François from a French Book of Hours, Brittany, c. 1504.

myrrh, used to anoint corpses, underlined the saving nature of his death.

The wise men were not Jews but Gentiles, underlining the universal reach of the Christian gospel, an aspect with which Matthew concludes his Gospel. Writing towards the end of the first century, Luke also saw clearly that the Christian message had very clear universal implications. It was 'good news' for all men and women.

Two Visits to Jerusalem

The Jewish law required Jesus' parents to take him to the Temple shortly after birth so that several purification ceremonies could be performed. Twelve years later Jesus paid another visit to Jerusalem, and quizzed the religious teachers there about the Jewish faith.

Mary and Joseph were devout Jews, so Jesus was circumcised and named eight days after he was born at the Temple in Jerusalem. Jewish convention dictated that two offerings had to be made at this time:

◆ A woman was ritually unclean for 40 days after giving birth and she had to make the appropriate offering before she could be restored to full communal life.
◆ A further offering of a pair of doves or two young pigeons was made to 'buy back' the firstborn in the family from God.

The first visit

The main purpose of taking Jesus to the Temple was to 'present' him to God. Two venerable Temple worshippers, Simeon and Anna, blessed Jesus and offered his future work joyfully to God. In a song, the Nunc Dimittis, Simeon prophesied that the gospel message was to be for all people, a note frequently picked up and echoed by Luke.

The second visit

Rabbinical teachers gathered daily in the outer precincts of the Temple (the Court of the Gentiles) to give instruction to their own disciples who sat, literally, at their feet. Jesus was to spend some time teaching his disciples, and others, in this place at the very end of his ministry. The visit that the young Jesus paid to the Temple, at the age of 12, was to mark the annual celebration of the festival of Passover. At the age of 13 Jewish boys were regarded as having attained spiritual maturity, as they are today, and it is likely that Jesus' parents were introducing him to the Temple in preparation for his own coming of age the following year.

Luke had another reason for recording this particular incident. Although he was still a child Jesus obviously had an extraordinary knowledge of and

The visit paid to the Temple in Jerusalem by the infant Jesus and his parents is the only incident recorded in the Gospels between the infancy narratives and the emergence of Jesus into public adult life.

When he was eight days old, Jesus was brought to the Temple to be circumcised and named according to the Jewish law. *The Circumcision* by Giovanni Bellini (c. 1430–1516).

insight into the Jewish scriptures. So great was this understanding that Jesus amazed the Jewish elders and scribes – a group specially trained in the intricacies of the Jewish law – with his erudition. The point of the story is made

Then Jesus went down to Nazareth with them and was obedient to them. But his mother treasured all these things in her heart. And Jesus grew in wisdom and stature and in favour with God and men.

LUKE 2:51–52

when Jesus' distraught parents find their missing son. Jesus asks them, 'Did you not know that I must be in my Father's house?' Already, in Luke's Gospel, Jesus demonstrates his awareness of his intimate relationship with God, his Father.

In spite of this, however, Jesus was still the dutiful child who returned home with his parents and was obedient to them. In the years that followed Jesus grew in spiritual wisdom and understanding.

57

Christ Among the Apostles from a mid-13th century psalter, possibly made for the Duchess of Breslau.

Jesus' public ministry began appropriately with his baptism by John the Baptist, since this was the occasion when he received confirmation of his divine status from God. His conflict with the powers of darkness, set to continue throughout his life, began with the satanically inspired temptations that Jesus experienced immediately after his baptism. Shortly afterwards he chose the 12 disciples who were to share the rest of his ministry with him and were to become the bedrock on which the Christian Church was built after his death.

The miracles that Jesus performed were scattered throughout his ministry and were a major element in his struggle with the powers opposed to the purposes of God. Disease, sickness, evil spirits and the unruly elements of nature were all symptoms of the tight grip which these sinister powers had upon human life. Each time that Jesus confronted them and emerged victorious, it pointed not only to the truth of his belief that he was God's chosen Messiah, but also underlined the message that the final defeat of such powers was only a matter of time. That final defeat was to come with the death of Jesus at Calvary.

Now, there was about this time, Jesus, a wise man... he was a doer of wonderful works, a teacher of such men as receive the truth with pleasure.

FLAVIUS JOSEPHUS (37–c. 95 CE),
JEWISH HISTORIAN

THE MINISTRY BEGINS

Contents

The Baptism of Jesus

All three Synoptic Gospels agree that the baptism of Jesus was the start of his public ministry. It was the occasion when God's witness to Jesus, his Son, was set as a seal on his future ministry.

Mark tells us that many people from the province of Judea and the city of Jerusalem went out to listen to John the Baptist and to be baptized by him. It was there that Jesus arrived, out of years of obscurity, on the banks of the River Jordan and asked John to baptize him. After doing so John largely disappeared from the story, only reappearing when Mark describes, at some length, his death at the hands of Herod. Matthew, Mark and Luke link the baptism of Jesus with his subsequent temptations in the wilderness, accounts of which follow directly afterwards.

Jesus is baptized

The irony of Jesus, the sinless Son of God, asking to be baptized for the forgiveness of his sins struck both Matthew and Luke as needing some explanation, but the same thought did not occur to Mark. For him, the importance of the episode lies in what happened directly afterwards. In his strikingly brief account he

As Jesus was praying, heaven was opened and the Holy Spirit descended on him in bodily form like a dove. And a voice came from heaven: 'You are my Son, whom I love; with you I am well pleased.'

LUKE 3:22

presents us with just three pieces of information, all of which are highly significant:

◆ 'As soon as Jesus came up out of the water, he saw heaven opening.' Jews believed that the sky was a great dome stretched out over the earth with a number of hierarchically arranged kingdoms above it – God's kingdom being the highest of all. When Jesus came up out of the water, he alone

IN JOHN'S GOSPEL

John does not describe Jesus' baptism in his Gospel. However, he does describe how God told him, 'The man on whom you see the Spirit come down and remain is he who will baptize with the Holy Spirit,' to which John responded, 'I have seen and I testify that this is the Son of God.'

The baptism of Jesus by John the Baptist was immediately followed by 40 days in the wilderness. *Baptism of Christ* by the Master of Female Half-Lengths (active 1500–30).

saw the heavens split wide open above him, suggesting that this was probably a personal vision rather than an external event that everyone witnessed.

◆ Then Jesus saw 'the Spirit coming down on him like a dove'. Jews believed that the Holy Spirit had been active since the creation of the world, carrying out God's will and inspiring the prophets of old to speak in the divine name. After his baptism the Holy Spirit came down on Jesus 'like a dove' to commission him for the work that lay ahead. Jesus now had the power and authority to act and speak in God's name.

◆ 'And a voice came from heaven, "You are my own dear Son, I am pleased with you."' These words, taken from Psalm 2:7 and Isaiah 42:1, underline the Christian belief that Jesus is God's Son – a belief affirmed here by God.

The baptism was a key event in Jesus' life, emphasizing the special relationship that he had with God his Father and the Holy Spirit – a relationship which was to form the bedrock of his ministry. God, for the first time, acknowledged that Jesus was his Son and this was immediately put to the test by the temptations that followed.

The Temptations of Jesus

Each Synoptic Gospel includes an account of the temptations of Jesus at the hands of Satan. As with many other events in the Gospels it is the significance of what happened, rather than its historical detail, that is important.

The hostile landscape of the Judean Desert. It was in this wilderness that Satan confronted Jesus in an attempt to deflect him from the task that God had given him.

The baptism of Jesus was followed by a time spent in the desert where, the Synoptic Gospels agree, he was tempted by Satan. Satan was a familiar figure to Jews, since in the Old Testament book of Job he was given God's permission to test Job almost beyond the point of human endurance. In tempting Jesus Satan was hoping to divert him from his future role as God's Messiah.

The temptations

The three temptations of Jesus take place in the desert – the location in which John the Baptist had spent much of his life baptizing and in which, it was popularly believed, malevolent demons and spirits held sway. The 40 days that Jesus spent fasting in this inhospitable place echoes the 40 years that the Israelites spent wandering in the wilderness before reaching the Promised Land of Canaan.

Mark's account of the

When Mark wrote his Gospel the Christians were in the middle of their first real bout of persecution. It must have encouraged them greatly to know that Jesus, the strong Son of God, had resisted all attempts by Satan to persuade him to take the easy way out. For them that would have been to abandon their Christian faith.

temptations is extremely brief and does not mention the individual temptations. Matthew and Luke provide us with more detail. Although they reverse the second and third temptations they agree on their nature and how Jesus resisted them:

◆ The first temptation is to turn stones into bread. The temptation's attraction was for him to use his divine power to meet his own material needs.

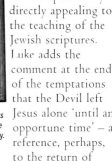

Christ Prays in the Wilderness from *Meditations on the Life of Christ*, Italian, 14th century.

◆ The second temptation is to throw himself down from the pinnacle of the Temple in Jerusalem. Jesus was being reminded of the promise of God's providential care in the scriptures and invited to test it unnecessarily.

◆ The third temptation is to worship Satan. Jesus is told that he will inherit all the kingdoms of the world if he offers Satan the worship due to God alone.

The Synoptic Gospels agree that Jesus countered each temptation by directly appealing to the teaching of the Jewish scriptures. Luke adds the comment at the end of the temptations that the Devil left Jesus alone 'until an opportune time' — a reference, perhaps, to the return of Satan to test him further as his death approached in the Garden of Gethsemane.

UNDERSTANDING THE TEMPTATIONS

It is, of course, perfectly possible to understand the temptations of Jesus as historical events. Some commentators, however, look at the allusions to ascent in the temptations — the pinnacle of the Temple and the kingdoms of the world viewed from a great height — and see these as indicating a visionary experience.

Jesus and his Disciples

At the beginning of his public ministry Jesus deliberately chose 12 disciples to share his life – to be with him, to preach and to drive out demons.

The Gospels describe the call of Jesus to seven disciples ('pupils') who then committed themselves to someone whom they clearly believed to be a rabbi (teacher). Jesus chose 12 disciples in all to form a close-knit and itinerant group; there were also many others who believed the message Jesus was preaching.

Jesus calls the disciples

Andrew was a disciple of John the Baptist when Jesus walked by and it was the Baptist who pointed him out as the Messiah. Andrew told his brother Simon what John had

A significant moment in Peter's life came when he hauled in an unusually large catch of fish, following Jesus' instructions. Peter realized he was in the presence of someone quite extraordinary. *The Miraculous Draft of Fishes* by Raphael (1483–1520).

said and he, too, became a disciple of Jesus. Jesus himself later changed Simon's name to Peter – 'the rock' – and he became the most prominent of the disciples and the first leader of the Christian Church. The next day, in Galilee, Philip and Nathaniel also heard the call of Jesus and became disciples.

Both Simon and Andrew were fishermen, as were James and John, two others who were called by Jesus to follow him when he saw them fishing on the Sea of Galilee. He challenged them to join him and become 'fishers of men'. Luke adds at this point the story of the miraculous catch of fish which Peter experienced and how this led to Peter confessing his sins: 'Go away from me Lord, for I am a sinful man.' The call of one other disciple is described in the Gospels – that of Matthew, the Jewish tax collector who worked for the Romans. To this small group Jesus later added five more.

Mark calls the 12 disciples 'apostles' (those who were 'sent'), but this title was only generally given to them after the upheaval of the Day of Pentecost. Three of the disciples – Peter, James and John – shared the most important moments in the life of Jesus and they were clearly special to him.

Why did Jesus choose 12 disciples? The number 12 was significant to all his Jewish followers. The Jewish nation was based on the 12 tribes named after the 12 sons of Jacob, one of the Jewish father-figures. It thus appeared to many that Jesus had taken the first step towards replacing the Jewish nation with the Christian Church which was to be based on the work of the 12 disciples.

Happy are they who know that discipleship simply means the life which springs from grace, and that grace simply means discipleship.

DIETRICH BONHOEFFER (1905–45), GERMAN LUTHERAN PASTOR

The role of the disciples

Mark tells us that Jesus chose his 12 disciples for three main reasons:

◆ To be with him. Jesus spent much of his time teaching his disciples about the kingdom of God so that they could pass his message on after he was gone.
◆ To preach. Although his healing work was important it was his preaching and teaching which were central to Jesus' mission. This work was continued by the disciples and the whole Christian Church after his death.
◆ To drive out demons. The disciples shared with Jesus God's authority to wage a continual war against the powers of darkness and to heal the sick. Many Christians believe that this should be an essential part of the Church's mission in the modern world.

Jesus and Miracles

Although many people were thought to be miracle-workers in first-century Palestine, Jesus was different. His miracles were a secondary part of his ministry, demonstrating that God was active and working through him.

Jesus was not, by any means, the only person in first-century Palestine performing 'miracles'. Greek, Roman and Jewish documents of the time show that 'miracles' were comparatively commonplace and widely accepted. Such miracle-workers usually chanted some kind of magical formula or ritual over the person in need before performing an exorcism. The inclusion of many miracles in the Gospels, therefore, would not have been surprising to first-century readers – it would have been expected.

Even Jesus' enemies accepted that he could, and did, perform miracles. They could not bring themselves, however, to believe that he did so by the power of the Holy Spirit. They preferred to attribute his power to Satan. This disagreement over the source of Jesus' power led to one of his earliest clashes with the religious authorities.

Miracles in the Gospels

Although there are as many as 35 miracles recorded in the Gospels they are not given particular prominence. It is worth remembering that there were times when Jesus refused to perform a miracle, or sign, in case it drew attention to himself for the wrong reason. It is as if he rationed his miracles so that people would see that he was not just a miracle-worker but someone who had a mission from God. Performing miracles was just one part of that mission. On many occasions Jesus commanded the people he healed not to tell others about it.

Jesus usually performed a miracle because he was moved with pity by the condition of those in need, or because they demonstrated extraordinary or unexpected faith. Faith was an essential requirement for Jesus

A miracle is not the breaking of laws of the fallen world, it is the re-establishment of the laws of the kingdom.

METROPOLITAN ANTHONY
OF SOUROZH, RUSSIAN-BORN
ORTHODOX MONK AND BISHOP

The first miraculous sign recorded by John in his Gospel was at a wedding, when Jesus turned water into wine. *Marriage at Cana* from *Meditations on the Life of Christ*, Italian, 14th century.

to perform miracle – either faith from the person concerned or, occasionally, from other people.

The miracles of Jesus owed nothing to sorcery or magic. At no time did Jesus try to compete with the contemporary miracle-workers by using a magical formula or esoteric language to achieve his ends. Jesus often touched the person in need with his hands, but it was usually Jesus' own word of command that actually brought about the miracle.

The 'mighty works' of Jesus cannot be separated from his teaching, and his miracles were often described in such a way as to draw attention to a spiritual truth. For example, the story of Jesus driving out an evil spirit from a man in the synagogue at Capernaum underlines the spiritual authority which made Jesus stand out from the teachers of the law as well as from other contemporary miracle-workers

The Healing Miracles

The most prominent of Jesus' miracles are those in which he healed people suffering from a wide range of illnesses. Often Jesus broke the social and religious conventions of the time by touching these people before healing them.

The most widely accepted explanation for sickness and disease in the time of Jesus was that they were the result of the activities of demons and evil spirits. For this reason it is not always easy to distinguish between a healing and an exorcism in the Gospels.

The healing work of Jesus

Faith-healers enjoyed considerable popularity in first-century Palestine by employing a mixture of spells, incantations and potions in their work. There is no suggestion in the Gospels that Jesus used such ritual magic. Instead, he would establish a

The healing of a blind man in Bethsaida is unique among the recorded miracles of Jesus. It is the only one that takes place in two stages – partially after Jesus applied saliva to the man's eyes and totally when he laid hands upon him.

physical bond between himself and the person needing help, either touching them briefly or laying his hands on their head or shoulders. When this involved contact with a person with leprosy, often called 'a dreaded skin disease' in the Gospels, Jesus broke a whole range of social and religious conventions.

On one occasion a woman with a haemorrhage was cured by simply touching Jesus' clothing, but this was very unusual. In his description of this event Mark reveals the poor reputation enjoyed by the medical profession at the time when he comments that the woman had spent all of her money seeking a cure but had only grown worse. Luke tells us that Jesus felt power go out of him when he cured a person and this was how he knew that the woman had touched him and been healed, even though he was surrounded by a crowd. The same power was linked with the Old Testament prophets, demonstrating that Jesus stood in the established prophetic tradition expected of the Messiah.

Jesus often healed solely by the sound of his voice. To a man with leprosy he simply said, 'Be made clean'; to a man with a shrivelled hand in the

Jesus never used spells or incantations in the course of healing the sick. Most often all that was required was a touch or a command. Healing the Woman with the Issue of Blood by Veronese (Paolo Caliari), (1528–88).

There is no difference between the words and works of Jesus. The works have exactly the same message as the words. The message and words concentrate on the announcement of the kingdom of God. The miracles and works show us what the kingdom is like.

JOHN WIMBER, CHARISMATIC LEADER OF THE 'SIGNS AND WONDERS' MOVEMENT

synagogue, he said, 'Stretch out your hand'; and to the paralysed man who was lowered through the roof by his four friends, he said, 'Stand up and take up your bed and walk.' Jesus did not even need to enter the house of a Roman centurion, but instead healed the centurion's servant with a word from a distance, as the man himself had suggested. On many occasions, however, Jesus' words and his touch went together to show that there was a spiritual lesson to be learned beyond the physical healing.

Exorcisms

The most controversial aspect of Jesus' healing ministry was the casting out of demons – exorcisms. There were three separate occasions in the Gospels when this happened.

The limited medical knowledge available in first-century Palestine meant that all forms of severe mental illness were simply classified as 'demonic possession'. The people afflicted turned to exorcists when they could find no comfort from recognized medical practitioners.

Jesus and exorcism

There are many references in the Gospels to evil spirits and demons, with three recorded instances of demonic possession, each with similar physical symptoms:

◆ In the instance of a man with an evil spirit, the spirit recognized Jesus: 'I know who you are – the Holy One of God'. When Jesus ordered him out of the man it threw him into a convulsive fit. The people were amazed because this confrontation between Jesus and the spirit added considerable authority to his teaching.

◆ In the story of a boy with an evil spirit, the boy was thrown to the ground foaming at the mouth, gnashing his teeth and becoming rigid whenever the spirit took control of him – the classic symptoms of what would be recognized today as an epileptic fit. The child was originally brought to the disciples but they could do nothing to help him.

◆ In the tale of a Gadarene demoniac, this man lived naked

> *When a man believed himself to be possessed he was 'conscious of himself and also of another being who constrained and controlled him from within'. That explains why the demon-possessed in Palestine so often cried out when they met Jesus. They knew that Jesus was believed by some at least to be the Messiah; they knew that the reign of the Messiah was the end of demons; and the man who believed himself to be possessed by a demon spoke as a demon when he came into the presence of Jesus.*
>
> WILLIAM BARCLAY,
> SCOTTISH THEOLOGIAN,
> WRITER AND BROADCASTER

Jesus regarded demons as agents of Satan (Lucifer), whose downfall he had witnessed. 'I saw Satan fall like lightning from heaven,' he told his disciples. *Lucifer's Presumption and Fall* from the Anglo-Saxon Caedmon manuscript, c. 1000.

in a graveyard and possessed some kind of superhuman strength so that no chains or fetters could hold him.

Understanding the exorcisms

The main feature of these three stories is that it was Jesus' words – 'Come out' – that brought deliverance to the individuals affected. This made his approach different from

that of contemporary exorcists. Jesus regarded the evil spirits that lived in these wretched people as the agents of Satan, the Prince of Darkness, and exorcism as part of the conflict in which he was engaged throughout his ministry – the work of casting out demons was expected of God's Messiah. The power of darkness loosed its grip on humanity as the kingdom of God that Jesus proclaimed began to win over people's hearts and minds.

A strange feature of the description of the three exorcisms is that the evil spirits recognized just who Jesus was – the 'Holy One of God', the Messiah – long before the disciples did. The same spirits were terrified by his power over them, since the tyranny which they had exercised over those they possessed was now broken. Jesus dealt with them ruthlessly; in the case of the Gadarene demoniac he sent the evil spirits into a herd of pigs which rushed headlong over a cliff.

Feeding the Hungry

The feeding of a crowd of more than 5,000 people by Jesus with just a few loaves and fish is the only miracle included in all four Gospels, indicating that it had considerable significance for the early Christian Church. In addition, Matthew and Mark provide accounts of an almost identical second miracle, although on this occasion the recorded crowd is smaller.

After returning from a tiring preaching mission Jesus took his disciples away on their own to rest, but they were followed by a crowd desperate to hear him teach. By late evening Jesus felt sorry for the hungry crowd far from home, and fed them miraculously using just five small barley loaves and two dried, salted fish.

JOHN AND THE FEEDING OF THE CROWD

In John's Gospel the miracle happened during the Jewish festival of Passover when all Jews celebrate the deliverance of their ancestors from Egyptian slavery by eating a communal meal. The manna the Israelites ate in the desert was, like all food, only 'temporary', but the 'food' that Jesus gives is eternal – the true bread from heaven.

Details of a miracle

It seems that the Gospel-writers had a largely Jewish readership in mind when they included this miracle. The crowd are described as 'sheep without a shepherd', a familiar phrase used in the Jewish scriptures to describe the nation of Israel. The details of the miracle are also very precise: the 12 baskets of leftovers collected after the people had finished eating are reminiscent of the 12 tribes of Israel.

Feeding the 4,000

The feeding of the 4,000 appears to have taken place in or around the Gentile area of the Decapolis, suggesting that this miracle and the feeding of the 5,000 are symbolically pointing in different directions. In one it is a Gentile crowd and in the other a largely Jewish audience who have their spiritual and their physical

Although we call this miracle the 'feeding of the 5,000' Matthew was emphatic that far more people were fed: 'The number of those who ate was about 5,000 men, besides women and children.'

The multiplication by Jesus of a boy's lunch of five loaves and two fish is remembered in this mosaic from the Church of Multiplication at Tabgha, Galilee.

hunger satisfied by Jesus in the kingdom of God.

A deeper meaning

The Gospel-writers clearly saw a deeper significance in the feeding miracles of Jesus than in any of his other 'mighty acts'. Two events, one from the Jewish scriptures and the other from the worship of the early Church, probably occupied their thoughts. First, there was the miraculous provision of food (manna) which Moses was able to negotiate with God for the Israelites while they were travelling to the Promised Land of Canaan. Both this and the miraculous feeding have a wilderness setting. Second,

before feeding the large crowd Jesus took the bread, blessed it, broke it and distributed it to the people. He did exactly the same with the bread that was on the table at his Last Supper with his disciples and this, in turn, provided the basis for the service of Communion in the early Church.

Controlling Nature

Two of Jesus' miracles – calming a storm and walking on water – show that he was believed to have supernatural power over the unruly forces of nature. Jews believed that such powers were a sign of divinity.

Sudden storms were very common on the inland Sea of Galilee, where the winds were funnelled between the surrounding hills. The storms in these two incidents must have been very severe because, as Luke's Gospel reports, they caused even seasoned fishermen, who knew the area well, to panic.

Calming the storm

Mark's version of Jesus calming a storm seems to have come from an eyewitness account, for he provides a vivid description of the storm and Jesus asleep in the stern of the boat with his head on a pillow. The disciples were travelling with him from one side of the lake to the other. The account draws a powerful contrast between the calmness of Jesus, the chaos of the storm and the panic of the disciples.

The command that Jesus issued to the waves and the storm is similar to that given to the evil spirit in Mark's Gospel: 'Quiet! Be still!' This similarity may suggest a belief that storms

were caused by evil spirits. The point of the story, apart from its

The disciples were astonished when Jesus calmed a violent storm with a single command. 'Who is this?' they asked. 'Even the winds and waves obey him!' *The Storm on the Sea of Galilee* by Rembrandt van Rijn (1606–69).

demonstration that Jesus had divine power over nature, is the recorded reaction of the disciples: 'Who is this? Even the winds and the waves obey him.' They knew of many passages in the scriptures which stated that only God had control over the waters of the sea.

Walking on the water

John suggests in his Gospel that after Jesus had fed the 5,000 people they tried to make him their king. Jesus went away from the crowd to pray and sent his disciples ahead of him by boat. While he was praying Jesus saw his disciples in the distance struggling to keep afloat in another of the storms which were so familiar on the Sea of Galilee.

Matthew and Mark, in their descriptions of the event, tell us that Jesus walked across the sea towards the boat. Matthew adds the detail that when Peter realized who it was walking on the water he leapt out of the boat and began to walk towards Jesus. He soon began to sink, however, and was only saved when Jesus reached out his hand to him. As soon as Jesus reached the boat the wind died down and the people were amazed, saying, 'Truly you are the Son of God.'

We can see why these

Lord God Almighty, none is as mighty as you; in all things you are faithful, O Lord. You rule over the powerful sea; you calm its angry waves... When the waters saw you, O God, they were afraid... You walked through the waves; you crossed the deep sea, but your footprints could not be seen.

PSALM 89:8–9; 77:16, 19

miracles were highly prized by the early Christians. The Jewish scriptures made it clear that God alone had the power and authority to calm the unruly elements of nature. The Jews were not a seafaring nation and the sea held many terrors for them. This was a particularly important message at a time when the Church was undergoing a long spell of persecution; to know that God was in control of everything was very comforting.

Raising the Dead

There were three occasions when Jesus brought someone back to life. Power to raise the dead was a true sign of the promised Messiah

The first raising from the dead is recorded by all three Synoptic Gospels, while the other two are found in Luke's Gospel and John's Gospel.

Raising Jairus' daughter

Jairus was a well-respected Jewish leader who arranged daily acts of worship in his local synagogue. When his daughter fell ill Jairus was uncertain about seeking Jesus' help because Jesus was often in conflict with people like himself, but by this time he was desperate. On his journey home with Jesus they were interrupted by someone else seeking help, and before long news reached them that Jairus' daughter had died. By the time the two of them reached Jairus' house professional mourners, a feature of every Jewish funeral, had already moved in.

Jesus' words to the gathered crowd – that the girl was not dead but only sleeping – suggest that he shared the common view that the experience of death was similar to that of a deep sleep. Only Peter, James and John and the child's parents were present when Jesus took the girl by the hand and spoke the Aramaic words which her mother might well have used to wake her each morning: '*Talitha koum!*' ('Little girl, I say to you, get up!'). The witnesses were sworn to secrecy.

Raising the widow's son

Only Luke records this very sad event. When a widow lost her only son it meant that she would have no means of support in her old age. Significantly Jesus touched the child's coffin, which would have rendered him 'ritually unclean'. The response of the people to the miracle showed that they recognized that the expected Messiah would be able to bring the dead back to life: 'A great prophet has appeared among us… God has come to help his people.'

Raising Lazarus

Only John's Gospel records this story. Mary, Martha and Lazarus, who lived in Bethany, were friends of Jesus. When Jesus arrived at their house Lazarus

By raising the dead Jesus was deliberately linking himself with the great prophetic figures of Elijah and Elisha in the Old Testament. It is interesting that both of these figures also raised a widow's son to life.

had been in his tomb for four days. Nevertheless, Jesus ordered that the stone sealing the tomb's entrance should be removed. In a loud voice Jesus called Lazarus from the tomb and he emerged with the grave clothes still wrapped around his body and face.

Clearly, the raising of Lazarus is the most remarkable example of Jesus raising the dead. Typically in John's Gospel it becomes the occasion for a deep theological reflection, this time on life, death and eternal life. Because the miracle occurred so close to the death and

I am the resurrection and the life. He who believes in me will live, even though he dies; and whoever lives and believes in me will never die.

JOHN 11:25–26

resurrection of Jesus himself, Christians inevitably saw in the event a foreshadowing of what was to take place so soon afterwards in Jerusalem.

Jesus delayed a journey to Bethany following a request to go there to heal his friend Lazarus. By the time Jesus arrived, Lazarus was dead. But he turned what could have been a miraculous healing into an opportunity to demonstrate God's power to raise the dead. *The Raising of Lazarus* (detail) by Sebastiano del Piombo (c. 1485–1547).

It was Jesus' teaching, more than anything else, that made his ministry unique. Jesus' listeners recognized the authority with which he spoke early on – he was not simply reinforcing past religious traditions but offering a new way of understanding God. At the heart of his message was the kingdom of God – a spiritual kingdom that was open to everyone.

This new kingdom was full of surprises, not least because the social outcasts and sinners gained entrance ahead of outwardly decent and respectable people. Jesus emphasized this message in many of his parables, which helped bring about a rift with the religious leaders of his time. They tried to separate themselves from all that was thought to be spiritually defiling, whereas Jesus drew alongside those in need of comfort and support.

For those capable of discerning the truth, the life and teaching of Jesus

The Last Supper (detail) by Fra Angelico (c. 1387–1455).

revealed clearly who he was. He was the Son of God, but his own favourite self-description was the 'Son of man'. Jesus identified himself totally with those he came to serve. He also knew himself to be the Jewish Messiah, but so many misunderstandings surrounded this title that Jesus was unwilling to accept it without reservation.

Our Lord did not invent the codex of canon law. He did not dictate the Summa *of Thomas Aquinas. He sat upon a hillside, perched himself in a rocking boat just off the beach. He spoke in the synagogues and in the houses of the people. The images he used were the simplest images of rural life.*

MORRIS WEST,
ROMAN CATHOLIC NOVELIST

JESUS THE TEACHER

Contents

The Parables of Jesus

The parables that Jesus told were central to his teaching about the kingdom of God.

It is not as easy as you might think to define the word 'parable'. The Greek word from which it is derived means 'to set two things side by side', so offering a comparison. In the time of Jesus, however, the word could also mean a proverb, an allusion or a prophetic oracle. Generally, a parable in the Gospels is introduced by the words 'The kingdom of God is like…' so teasing out a comparison. Jesus mainly used parables to explain the nature of this kingdom.

The purpose of parables

Jesus told parables for a variety of reasons, but he was mainly concerned to increase the understanding of his listeners about the kingdom of God. He wanted to provoke them into thinking about this kingdom, so he did not usually offer to explain the meaning of a parable. The parable of the sower in Mark's Gospel is a notable exception to the rule. This parable is based on a familiar sight in first-century Palestine – the sower sowing seed all around him as he walks up and down his fields. However, the parable is much more concerned with the nature of the soil into which the seed falls than it is with the sower himself. The soil provides an analogy for understanding how people hear and respond to the 'sowing of the seed' – the message of God's salvation.

The parables, Jesus said, were given to ordinary people so that 'they may be ever seeing

PARABLES AND THE TEACHING OF JESUS

The parables of Jesus concentrate on the kingdom of God, but they also illuminate many other themes, including the demands of discipleship, prayer and the right use of wealth and possessions. Jesus used parables frequently because they caught the attention of his listeners; were instantly memorable; challenged the assumptions that people held about God; encouraged them to look at life from a different perspective; and provoked them into further, deeper, reflection.

Although it contains passages that share some of the characteristics of the parables – such as the good shepherd and the vine and the branches – there are no parables in John's Gospel.

Jesus told the parable of the good Samaritan in response to the question, 'Who is my neighbour?'

A parable is... an assault on the conventions, including the social, economic, and mythic structures that people build for their own comfort and security. A parable is a story meant to invert and subvert these structures and to suggest that the way of the kingdom is not the way of the world.

SALLIE McFAGUE,
NORTH AMERICAN THEOLOGIAN

parables in order to hide the truth rather than make it clearer. Yet the evidence suggests that for anyone prepared to listen, the parables do make it quite clear who does and who does not belong to God's kingdom.

but never perceiving, and ever hearing but never understanding; otherwise they might turn and be forgiven'. This seems a very harsh statement and appears to suggest that Jesus spoke in

The Kingdom of God

The kingdom of God was at the heart of Jesus' teaching. It signified both the reign of God which had begun with the coming of Jesus, and the future rule of Jesus when the Messianic kingdom arrives.

When Matthew's Gospel speaks of the 'kingdom of heaven', as it often does, it means exactly the same as Mark and Luke's Gospels, when they speak of the 'kingdom of God'.

The first words of Jesus recorded in Mark's Gospel clarify the nature of his message: 'The right time has come and the kingdom of God is near! Turn away from your sins and believe the good news!' People were told to have faith in the gospel which announced that God's kingdom had arrived with Jesus. This kingdom was shown first in the life of Jesus and then in the lives of his followers.

The mystery of the kingdom

Mark was keen to show that the kingdom's arrival is silent, unnoticed by the majority of people, and that God chose to introduce this kingdom through a Messiah who suffered and died. This mystery forms the core of many of Jesus' parables.

Jesus explained how to enter this kingdom. He mixed freely with 'sinners', social outcasts despised by the righteous, and with tax collectors, who were regarded as collaborators with the Romans. To those who became upset by the company he kept Jesus told the parable of the prodigal son, in which the younger son represents all those who return to their father, God, for forgiveness, after living a life of debauchery and selfishness. They find forgiveness in God's kingdom.

> *The kingdom comes indeed as a gift but it comes also as a responsibility inviting urgent and active response from those to whom it is given. Salvation comes from God, but it is actualized in and through the struggles of the poor.*
>
> GEORGE M. SOARES-PRABHU,
> INDIAN NEW TESTAMENT
> SCHOLAR

GOD'S KINGDOM AND JUDGMENT

Jesus did not say that God's kingdom had come, only that it was close at hand. This kingdom is growing on earth, just as corn seed grows into a plant before it is harvested. Similarly, the kingdom of God grows until God gathers in the harvest. Then will be the time of judgment. This is the theme of several parables, such as that of the sheep and goats, in Matthew's Gospel, which sets out the future criteria for judgment. In helping others in need, people are helping Jesus and it is on this that God will judge them. Those who have helped others (the sheep) will be rewarded with the gift of eternal life; those who turned their backs on the needy (the goats) will suffer eternal punishment.

Last Judgment by Fra Angelico (c. 1387–1455).

Jesus used the example of a small child to show the spiritual simplicity which people needed to enter the kingdom. Just as a child depends on others for safety and provision, so anyone entering God's kingdom must depend totally on, and show faith in, God.

God the Father

Jesus inherited the idea of the fatherhood of God from his Jewish upbringing but developed it much further. It became his favourite way of speaking about his relationship with God.

Although other beliefs about God are more prominent in the Jewish scriptures, they speak on more than one occasion of God as the father of the Jewish nation. To Jesus, however, the term summed up almost everything about God that he had been sent to share with his listeners.

The faithfulness of God

Above all else, Jesus wanted to help people understand that God actively cares for the whole of his creation, for all human beings, whether good or sinful, and that such compassion must be present in any life that is to be pleasing to God. The care of God extends beyond the human world to the world of natural things – since the birds and flowers cannot look after themselves, so God needs to take care of them. The continuing beauty of the natural world shows how faithful God is in carrying this out.

Jesus compared God to a human father who is always alert to every opportunity to give his children what is best for them. Everyone can trust God to meet their earthly needs as long as they make it their first priority to enter his kingdom. It is the 'little ones' – not just children but those who share a childlike innocence – who are of such concern to the Father that he searches for them as a shepherd looks for his lost sheep, or as a poor woman turns her home over to find a missing coin.

Jesus and his Father

It was in the intimacy of prayer that Jesus addressed God most naturally as his Father:

◆ The unique relationship between Jesus and his Father in heaven is very apparent in his thanksgiving prayer recorded in Matthew's Gospel. Jesus says that special spiritual secrets have been given to him by God and that he then shares those secrets with his followers on earth.
◆ In the Garden of Gethsemane Jesus addresses God by the Aramaic word

The Pater Noster Church stands on the Mount of Olives on what is believed to be the site where Jesus gave the thanksgiving prayer to his disciples. On the walls of the church the Lord's Prayer, the paternoster, is written in 100 different languages.

All things have been committed to me by my Father. No one knows the Son except the Father, and no one knows the Father except the Son and those to whom the Son chooses to reveal him.

MATTHEW 11:27

'Abba', a word which indicated a very respectful relationship.

◆ In the two prayers recorded by Luke from the cross Jesus speaks to God as his Father.

◆ In the Lord's Prayer Jesus provided his followers with a model for their own prayers. It opens with the words, 'Our Father, who art in heaven…'

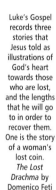

Luke's Gospel records three stories that Jesus told as illustrations of God's heart towards those who are lost, and the lengths that he will go to in order to recover them. One is the story of a woman's lost coin. *The Lost Drachma* by Domenico Feti (1589–1624).

The Holy Spirit

In the Old Testament the Holy Spirit was the power and activity of God in the world. In the Gospels the Holy Spirit was given to Jesus to empower him for his ministry, and, later, to all believers after Jesus had gone.

In the Old Testament the Spirit of God moved upon the primordial waters before the creation of the world, to bring creative order out of chaos. In the early days of Israel's history the same Spirit was the divine power given to individuals to perform extraordinary and heroic deeds or to speak prophetically in the divine name. For much of this time God's power was only dispensed by the Spirit on a temporary basis for a particular task, but by the time of such major prophets as Isaiah it was considered to be a permanent gift.

The Holy Spirit and Jesus

The work of the Holy Spirit is one of the dominant themes of Luke's Gospel. The Spirit is active in the Gospel from the beginning, working in the lives of Elizabeth and Zechariah, and with John the Baptist. The Holy Spirit was involved in the conception of Jesus and with Simeon as he blessed the infant Jesus in the

Temple. The Holy Spirit came upon Jesus at his baptism in a dove-like form and led him out into the wilderness to be tempted by Satan. The Holy

THE HOLY SPIRIT IN THE WORLD

In one sense the Holy Spirit had been in the world since its creation but, in another sense, he had yet to be given. Jesus told his disciples that it was a good thing that he was about to leave them so that the Holy Spirit – the Counsellor – could be given. He was coming to convict the world of sin, righteousness and judgment. The 'Spirit of Truth' would also guide everyone who believes into all truth. His role was clearly defined: 'He will speak on what he hears, and he will tell you what is to come. He will bring glory to me. He will bring glory to me by taking what is mine and making it known to you.'

The Spirit of the Lord is on me, because he has anointed me to preach good news to the poor. He has sent me to proclaim freedom for the prisoners, and recovery of sight for the blind, to release the oppressed, to proclaim the year of the Lord's favour.

LUKE 4:18–19

The Trinity – God in the form of three distinct persons: Father, Son and Holy Spirit – has always been beyond comprehension. *The Trinity* from a Flemish Book of Hours by the Master of the Prayer Book of Maximilian, after 1488.

a prophecy the Gospel-writer Matthew believed to be fulfilled in Jesus. Jesus possessed the Spirit fully because of his relationship with God, the Father, who gave him the Spirit 'without measure'. The earlier prophetic figures had received God's Spirit only in part. Jesus, on the other hand, was the perfect prophet living a life totally in keeping with the will of God.

Spirit provided Jesus with the necessary power for him to begin his ministry. The power and authority of God, in the form of the Holy Spirit, were with Jesus from the very beginning.

The prophet Isaiah had clearly foreseen that the one in whom God's Spirit permanently resided would have a unique Messianic role –

The Jewish Scriptures

Jesus quoted freely from the Jewish scriptures, affording them considerable, but not absolute, authority. The reason for this is that he saw himself as the living fulfilment of the scriptures and thus superior to them.

There are at least 40 direct quotations from the Jewish scriptures in the Gospels and a further 70 probable allusions to stories and teachings taken from them. The quotations are often introduced by the simple words: 'It is written…'

The authority of the scriptures

In public debate Jesus often used a quotation from the Jewish scriptures to settle an argument and this was effective because his Jewish listeners fully accepted their authority. The scriptures also provided the moral and spiritual

> Do not think that I have come to abolish the Law or the Prophets; I have not come to abolish them but to fulfil them. I tell you the truth, until heaven and earth disappear, not the smallest letter, not the least stroke of a pen, will by any means disappear from the Law until everything is accomplished.
>
> MATTHEW 5:17–18

JESUS THE TEACHER

Although not formally trained as a Jewish rabbi, Jesus was clearly accepted as an authoritative teacher by the people. As such he would have been expected to be extremely knowledgeable about the Jewish scriptures and to use them freely in his teaching. This is borne out in the Gospels where Jesus uses direct quotations and obscure allusions to the Jewish scriptures. The essential difference between him and the 'scribes' – whose task was to analyse and interpret the scriptures – was that he taught the people with 'authority'. This authority stemmed from the fact that he was perceived as a prophet – with a direct message from God – rather than a rabbi, whose role was to interpret the message already found in the scriptures.

A Jewish prayer book (*Haggadah Shil Pesach*) illustrating the story of the Passover in the Italian style, 1460 (shelfmark Or. 1404).

especially the Ten Commandments, in the Sermon on the Mount, although he felt free to reinterpret them in the light of the new revelation he had brought. His frequent complaint against the religious leaders of his time was that they often missed the important points of the scriptures because they were so wrapped up in safeguarding its detail.

The fulfilment of the Jewish scriptures

Jesus announced that he had come to fulfil the Jewish scriptures, not to destroy or abolish them. In his life, teaching and death he offered a way of understanding the scriptures that went beyond the surface to their inner meaning. In his conversation with two unnamed disciples after his resurrection, Luke tells us that 'beginning with Moses and all the prophets he explained to them what was said concerning himself in all the scriptures'. It was in this sense that he had come to fulfil the scriptures.

framework within which Jesus organized his own life – he turned to them, for instance, when he was being tempted by Satan in the wilderness. He also found solace in the Jewish scriptures when he was confronted by the agony of the last few hours of his life.

Jesus clearly accepted the authority of the scriptures when he was teaching his disciples. He depended heavily on the teachings of the Torah,

The Sermon on the Mount

The Sermon on the Mount is a special collection of sayings, parables and teachings of Jesus. It contains the essence of his teaching about the behaviour expected of those who belong to the kingdom of God.

In the Synoptic Gospels Jesus taught in short, pithy and memorable sayings or in parables, while in John's Gospel his teaching is cast in long, unbroken discourses. The Sermon on the Mount is almost certainly a collection of Jesus' sayings brought together by Matthew or someone else in the early Church.

The teaching of Jesus
The so-called Sermon on the Mount appears in

In the Sermon on the Mount, Jesus set out many of the radical principles involved in belonging to God's kingdom, which would have taken his listeners by suprise. *The Sermon on the Mount* (1442) by Fra Angelico (c. 1387–1455).

In Matthew's Gospel it is clear that Jesus delivers the Sermon on the Mount on a mountain. In his briefer account Luke refers to Jesus teaching on a level place, which many think may have been by the Sea of Galilee.

Matthew's Gospel, while a shorter parallel version, the 'Sermon on the Plain', is found in Luke's Gospel. A comparison of the two accounts suggests that they are both based on an earlier collection of sayings, either written or oral, which the two evangelists made use of. The collection may well have been brought together initially to provide a tool for the teaching of new converts to the faith.

The sermon is concerned with the nature of God's kingdom and the behaviour expected of those who belong to it. The Beatitudes, with which the Sermon begins, outline the spiritual characteristics which are, often unconsciously, displayed by members of the kingdom.

At the heart of the sermon is an explanation of the relationship between Jesus and the Jewish law. Explaining that he has come to fulfil the law, Jesus also underlines that he has come to unveil, for the first time, the true demands of the law. For instance, the law required a person not just to abstain from killing but from hatred itself; not just to avoid adultery but from harbouring any lustful thoughts; not just to repay others equally for their violence ('an eye for an eye and a tooth for a tooth') but to be

The Sermon on the Mount is a compass rather than an ordinance map; it gives direction rather than directions.

T.W. MANSON

nonviolent in both thought and action. Those who belong to God's kingdom are to strive for the very perfection which God himself shows.

Jesus also criticizes the hypocrisy which a show of outward piety often disguises. Almsgiving, prayer and fasting are important spiritual activities, but not if they are simply used to enhance a person's reputation for holiness. True purity of heart finds its own reward. God rewards those whose eyes are firmly set on building up 'treasure in heaven' and not 'treasures on earth'. To underline this point, Jesus set forward the so-called 'Golden Rule': 'In everything, do to others what you would have them do to you.' This is the guiding principle for all those who want to live their lives according to the rules of God's kingdom.

The Beatitudes

The Beatitudes are considered by many to be among the most sublime statements of true spirituality to be found in religious literature. They express the spiritual characteristics of the person entering God's kingdom and turn on its head much traditional teaching.

Although there is a lot of common ground between Matthew's account of the Beatitudes and Luke's there are also some significant differences:

◆ Matthew lists nine Beatitudes, but Luke only mentions four, plus four 'Woes' that Matthew does not mention.
◆ Matthew writes in the third person ('Blessed are those who…') while Luke writes in the second person ('Blessed are you…').
◆ Matthew describes the qualities of those who are part of God's kingdom; Luke, with his great interest in the poor and disadvantaged, writes more of those who enjoy little of this world's prosperity.

What the Beatitudes say
Following Matthew's account, the first four Beatitudes speak of a reversal in fortunes that belonging to God's kingdom will bring to the 'poor in spirit',

'those who mourn', 'the meek' and 'those who hunger and thirst for righteousness'. The

> *Blessed are the poor in spirit, for theirs is the kingdom of heaven.*
> *Blessed are those who mourn, for they will be comforted.*
> *Blessed are the meek, for they will inherit the earth.*
> *Blessed are those who hunger and thirst for righteousness, for they will be filled.*
> *Blessed are the merciful, for they will be shown mercy.*
> *Blessed are the pure in heart, for they will see God.*
> *Blessed are the peacemakers, for they will be called the sons of God.*
> *Blessed are those who are persecuted because of righteousness, for theirs is the kingdom of heaven.*
> *Blessed are you when people insult you, persecute you, and falsely say all kinds of evil against you because of me.*
>
> MATTHEW 5:3–11

Not only was Jesus' teaching radical, but his lifestyle was as well. Flouting social convention, fear and even Old Testament Law, he approached lepers and touched them in order to heal them. *Healing of the Ten Lepers* by James Tissot (1836–1902).

The remarkable thing about Jesus was that, although he came from the middle class and had no appreciable disadvantages himself, he mixed socially with the lowest of the low and identified himself with them. He became an outcast by choice.

ALBERT NOLAN,
SOUTH AFRICAN THEOLOGIAN

act on the words of Jesus in the light of the coming judgment. These words closely reflect the time and age in which Matthew was writing his Gospel (between 80 and 100 CE), when the Church had recently passed through a period of persecution at the hands of the Romans. To those who had suffered, the promise of the Beatitudes was that their reward in heaven would be great.

remainder of the Beatitudes speak of the rewards that will come in a kingdom, God's kingdom, that is yet to be fully realized, although both Matthew and Luke seem to suggest that the full disclosure of God's kingdom is close at hand.

The Beatitudes reach their climax with a call to people to

Prayer

Jesus clearly believed that prayer is a vital spiritual activity for those who belong to God's kingdom. He underlined this by setting his followers a clear example through giving prayer priority in his own life.

In the Sermon on the Mount Jesus not only encouraged his followers to pray in the right way, but also gave them a prayer – the Lord's Prayer – to use as their model. In the worldwide Christian Church this prayer remains the only one that is used universally throughout the many Churches and denominations.

> *Prayer is the sum of our relationship with God. We are what we pray. The degree of our faith is the degree of our prayer. Our ability to love is our ability to pray.*
>
> CARLO CARRETTO, SPIRITUAL WRITER

Teaching about prayer

As well as setting an example by praying before making any major decision, such as choosing his 12 disciples, Jesus also gave his followers some guidelines to help them pray:

◆ He told them to pray quietly in secret. As Jews often raised their arms when they prayed they could be seen performing such actions on street corners and in the Temple precincts.

THE LORD'S PRAYER

It was common for Jewish rabbis to teach their disciples a prayer for their own personal use. Both Luke and Matthew's Gospels have versions of the Lord's Prayer and the differences between them suggest that the prayer was not intended to be used in the early Church in the repetitive way that some Christians use it today. Luke's version of the prayer is the shorter. In both versions the prayer falls naturally into two parts:

◆ Adoration, beginning with the word 'Father', reminds us that for Jews a person's name signified their whole character. The prayer is that God may be honoured and worshipped and that his rule over the person's life may be accepted.

◆ Physical and spiritual needs, cast in a plural form, imply that this was a communal prayer. The prayer for the forgiveness of sins involves a confession of one's own shortcomings. The final request that there should be no 'hard testing' perhaps implies that the Christian community was expecting persecution.

◆ Jesus taught that private devotions should be performed in secret without using the long prayers for which the Gentiles were well known.

◆ Jesus encouraged them to expect God to answer. In his parable of a persistent widow

Our Father in heaven,
hallowed be your name,
your kingdom come,
your will be done,
on earth as it is in heaven.
Give us today our daily bread.
Forgive us our debts,
as we also have forgiven our debtors.
And lead us not into temptation,
but deliver us from the evil one.

MATTHEW 6:9–13

and a judge, the needs of the widow were met because she did not allow the judge any peace until he responded to her pleas! The judge may have been unwilling to listen to her but God, unlike the judge, is always ready and willing to answer those who pray to him.

◆ Jesus taught them to pray humbly. In the parable of the Pharisee and the tax collector the Pharisee demanded to have his prayers answered by God, while the tax collector could not think of any reason why God should listen to him. No need to ask whose prayers were answered!

Discipleship

Jesus spent much of his time teaching his followers how to be disciples. Discipleship involved living lives of commitment, self-giving and, for many of the early Christians, self-sacrifice.

In first-century Palestine people often attached themselves to outstanding and respected teachers to 'sit at their feet' and be taught by them. The Gospel-writers refer, for instance, to the disciples of the Pharisees, John the Baptist and Moses, and there were many other similar groups. The close and intimate relationship between teacher and pupil was a strong Jewish tradition. Jesus spent the bulk of his time with his disciples and the relationship between them was such that spiritual insights were revealed, communicated and interpreted freely.

The demands of discipleship

Unlike other teacher–pupil relationships, the Gospels make it clear that it was Jesus who chose his disciples – not the other way round. He 'called' them to leave their homes, friends and families, to join him in his itinerant ministry and to continue his work after he was gone. Whatever the cost might be their first priority was always their discipleship and commitment to Christ.

The demands made of the 12 disciples were also required of all would-be followers of Jesus. This is why some turned back when the cost was spelled out. A rich young ruler turned back when he realized that Jesus was calling him to give up everything, including his considerable wealth and possessions. Jesus told two other potential disciples that following him would cut across all normal human concerns, including ordinary family relationships.

Elsewhere Jesus spoke of the need for his followers to openly acknowledge their faith,

Contrary to the dominant attitude of our own society, one's economic life and standard of living is not a private matter. It is a critical issue of faith and discipleship.

JIM WALLIS, NORTH AMERICAN CHRISTIAN ACTIVIST

FEMALE FOLLOWERS OF JESUS

All of the 12 disciples were men but the Gospels make it clear that many women were among the early followers of Jesus. This was extremely unusual in the male-dominated Palestinian society of the first century. Some of these women travelled with Jesus on his teaching and healing tours. They also accompanied him at the end of his life to Jerusalem, were present at his crucifixion and were the first to arrive at the empty tomb on Easter morning. Luke also mentions a group of women who not only travelled with Jesus and his disciples but also provided much-needed financial support.

since the Son of man (Jesus) would do the same for all faithful witnesses before the angels of heaven and deny those who refused to openly identify themselves with him. The cost of such an open-ended commitment could be far-reaching. There was no room in the teaching of Jesus for secret discipleship. Jesus warned his followers that they could find themselves on trial for their faith, but they were encouraged not to be afraid.

The Son of God

The title 'Son of God', often given to Jesus in the Gospels, expresses his place in the Trinity and the closeness of his relationship with God, his Father.

Although 'Son of God' is not the title most often used of Jesus in the Gospels, Mark clearly believed that it summed up the real mystery of Jesus' ministry – God present on earth. It is there in the opening words of Mark's Gospel ('The beginning of the gospel about Jesus Christ, the Son of God'), and the Roman centurion's confession at the foot of the cross comes directly after the death of Jesus: 'Surely this man was the Son of God!' This confession acts as a kind of epitaph on the whole life and ministry of Jesus. As God's Son, Jesus had a special divinely bestowed role to play on earth and a unique relationship with God, his Father – as Matthew, Mark, Luke and John make clear in their Gospels.

Jesus, uniquely God's Son

The first clue to help us understand the meaning of the phrase 'Son of God' comes from the Old Testament. People who were close to God, and had a special relationship with him, were often described in the Old Testament as 'sons of God'. At different times in the Jewish scriptures the title was applied to the angels in heaven, the nation of Israel, judges and rulers.

When the title was given to Jesus it indicated that he was God's representative on earth, called by God to carry out a special mission. Jesus was not just one of many 'sons of God' in the old sense, for his relationship with God was unique and quite unlike that enjoyed by any human being – or angel! Jesus was *one* with God, Jesus *was* God. Even at the early age of 12 Jesus regarded the Temple in Jerusalem as 'my Father's house'.

The Son of God in the Gospels

At the beginning of his Gospel Mark presents Jesus as the one who has 'come' from God and, after death, he was the one who 'returned home' to his Father God in heaven. In between, during his time on earth as a human being, the special relationship that Jesus enjoyed with God visibly broke through

Simon Peter describes Jesus as 'the Son of the living God' in Matthew's Gospel. God himself says Jesus is his Son at Jesus' baptism. Evil spirits used the title too, and Jesus used it of himself more than once. Even the High Priest called Jesus the Son of God during Jesus' trial.

from time to time. Jesus was called God's Son on two special occasions: at his baptism and at his transfiguration.

The people who followed Jesus closely were amazed by the God-like qualities that they saw in him. Mark tells us that this happened after Jesus had:

◆ performed many miracles.
◆ taught in a way that was quite unlike that of any other teacher.

God... has only one answer to every human need — his Son, Jesus Christ.

WATCHMAN NEE (NEE TO-SHENG), CHINESE EVANGELIST

◆ shown himself to be God's Son.
◆ spoken with his disciples about future suffering.

On a number of occasions Jesus spoke of his relationship with God in a way that could only infer equality. His listeners fully understood the implications of what he said and charged him with blasphemy. *Eternal Image* (1998) by Serguei Orgunov.

The Son of Man

By referring to himself frequently as the 'Son of man' Jesus was stressing his own essential humanity. He was God on earth but his human nature was no illusion – it was real.

It is often necessary to go back to the Old Testament to explain some of the central ideas in the teaching of Jesus. This is certainly the case with the title 'Son of man'.

In the Old Testament
In the Old Testament, where the phrase was widely used, 'Son of man' carried two meanings:

◆ It described any member of the human race, a human being. In the book of Ezekiel, for instance, the phrase crops up no less than 93 times and each time the reference is to the prophet himself. God frequently addressed Ezekiel as 'mortal man' or 'Son of man' to stress his humanity, mortal and sinful, totally dependent on God.
◆ In the book of Daniel 'Son of man' refers to a glorious being who descended from heaven to reign on earth. This figure is superhuman, divine and eternal, one who has existed since the time before the world was created. The 'Son of man' remains hidden until the end of time when he emerges with his angels to judge the human race.

In the Gospels
The influence of the Jewish scriptures over Jesus can be clearly seen here. Quite often, he used the title 'Son of man' instead of the personal pronoun 'I' to refer to himself. At other times he used it, as Daniel did, to refer to his future coming on the clouds of heaven, an event to be followed by his own exaltation at God's right hand in heaven. This will happen as the world ends and a new time, God's time, begins.

Often, though, Jesus used the title in his own new, distinctive way. He referred to himself as the Son of man 14 times in Mark and on 11 of these occasions he was referring to his own forthcoming suffering and death. This new and striking idea was based on Isaiah's picture of God's suffering

In Jesus, God triumphed over human frailty. *The Creation of Man* by Marc Chagall (1887–1985).

servant, the Messiah, who would suffer and die to redeem sinful humanity. This comes out most clearly on the three occasions when Jesus spoke to his disciples about his death. No talk there of victory and triumph – only of suffering and death.

It is within this context that the Son of man is said to have the power to forgive sins. In the account of the healing of a paralysed man Jesus tells the man that his sins have been forgiven before he heals him. Jesus was both an ordinary man, sharing a common humanity with the rest of the human race, and yet he was special, sent by God and sharing divinity with his Father in heaven. It is these two aspects of Jesus which are conveyed by the titles 'Son of God' and 'Son of man'. Between them they sum up all that the Gospels say about Jesus.

On many occasions in the Gospels Jesus referred to himself as the 'Son of man' – it was his favourite self-designation. At no time, however, did anyone else apply the title to him.

The Messiah

'Messiah' and 'Christ' both mean the 'Anointed One' and refer to a figure who would set up God's everlasting kingdom of peace on earth. Christians believe that Jesus was anointed by God to inaugurate God's eternal kingdom.

The title 'Messiah' comes from the Old Testament, where it refers to someone who was anointed with oil by a priest or prophet before being sent out by God to perform a special task. Jews often applied it to the special king they were praying for, who would deliver them from all their enemies before establishing God's kingdom on earth. They believed that this king would be descended from King David, the second king of Israel from the 10th century BCE, who was considered by Jews to have been their perfect leader.

Jesus the Messiah

There is no recorded instance in the Gospels where Jesus expressly claimed to be the Messiah, but on three occasions other people responded to him as such:

◆ At Caesarea Philippi Jesus asked his disciples what they

Some people were disappointed by Jesus. They had hoped for a military leader who would establish a new Jewish state. Instead Jesus had come to bring about God's kingdom on earth. To some, his claim to be the Messiah was deserving only of stoning. *They Cast Stones at Him* by James Tissot (1836–1902).

The Gospels themselves make it clear that Jesus and his contemporaries were at cross-purposes when they spoke of the Messiah. To the Jews, the Messiah was to be a political king. For Jesus, being the Messiah meant humble service and obedience to God's will.

JOHN DRANE,
BRITISH WRITER

thought of him. Peter answered, 'You are the Messiah.' Jesus told him that he was 'blessed' to have been given this insight by God – he could not have arrived at it in any other way.

◆ On a road close to Jericho, a blind beggar, Bartimaeus, addressed Jesus as the 'Son of David' – an accepted reference to the Messiah. Onlookers told Bartimaeus to be silent but Jesus was happy to accept the title.

◆ At his trial before the Jewish authorities in the house of the High Priest, Jesus seemed to acknowledge that he was the Messiah.

A different kind of Messiah

It is clear that Jesus' reluctance to accept the title of Messiah was largely down to popular misunderstanding about its implications. Clearly, he was not the warrior-king that many Jews were expecting to drive the Romans out of Palestine. Instead, Jesus taught his followers to love their enemies and do good to those who hated them.

Jesus departed from current Jewish expectations in other ways as well. The Jews expected their Messiah to live a holy life separate from all defiling contact with others, but Jesus mixed freely with prostitutes and other social outcasts. They expected the Messiah to uphold the whole Law of Moses (the Torah), but Jesus suggested that the Law was not enough by itself and should not act as a great millstone around the necks of the people.

Largely because of these misunderstandings Jesus was reluctant to openly accept the title of Messiah. He was much more concerned about drawing people into the kingdom of God than he was in asserting his own Messiahship. He also wanted the people to understand that while he, as Messiah, had been sent by God to carry out a divine mission, that mission would inevitably lead to suffering and death. Moreover his mission as Messiah was not to Jews alone but to all people, Jews and Gentiles alike.

The shadow of the cross fell upon the last few months of Jesus' ministry. On a number of occasions he spoke of his impending death, but his disciples failed to take it in.

After Jesus' parents took him with them to Jerusalem at the age of 12 for the Passover the Synoptic Gospels do not record any further visit to the city until the final one that ended with his death. John's Gospel, however, suggests that Jesus frequently visited Jerusalem, especially to celebrate the main religious festivals. We do know that the city – known as Zion, the city of God – had a special place in Jesus' heart, as it did for all Jews.

On one occasion Jesus wept over the city and its inhabitants because he wanted to embrace all of its people, 'just as a hen gathers her chicks under her wings', but they would have none of it. Instead, as Jesus approached the city for the last time, he knew that ahead of him lay only rejection, suffering and death.

Beforehand, there were to be two important occasions on which the divine truth about Jesus broke through in moments of God-given revelation. First, the confession of faith by Peter at Caesarea Philippi in which he saw the truth about Jesus, the Messiah. This was immediately followed by his transfiguration in front of three of his disciples who, for a moment, became aware of the divinity which was invariably hidden behind his humanity. On this occasion God gave him the same endorsement which he had provided at his baptism.

O Jerusalem, Jerusalem, you who kill the prophets and stone those sent to you, how often have I longed to gather your children together, as a hen gathers her chicks under her wings, but you were not willing!

LUKE 13:34

TOWARDS DEATH

Contents

At Caesarea Philippi

Peter's confession of faith in Jesus at Caesarea Philippi
marks a watershed in the Gospel story. From this point
onwards the eyes of Jesus were very firmly set on reaching
Jerusalem – and death.

In Caesarea Philippi, an inland
city on the River Jordan,
stood a great temple built by
Herod the Great to honour
Caesar Augustus, the emperor
who had given the city to him.
It was Herod's son, Philip
the Tetrarch, who later named
the city after the emperor to
distinguish it from another
city of the same name on the
Mediterranean coast.

The questions of Jesus

Situated on the edge of Jewish
territory, Caesarea Philippi was
a quiet location from which
Jesus could launch out to
preach in the surrounding
villages without being mobbed
by those seeking his attention.
It was while he was on his way
to these villages that Jesus
asked his disciples two very
important questions.

The first question was,
'Tell me, who do the people
say that I am?' Although it
was very unusual for a rabbi
to ask questions directly of
his disciples, Jesus wanted his
closest friends to understand

more about him and his
mission. The answers they gave
were the same as those provided
earlier by Herod Antipas and
the people after John the
Baptist had been beheaded:
that Jesus was John the Baptist
brought back to life, Elijah or
one of the prophets. Elijah was
the greatest of the old Jewish
prophets who, it was believed,

The Messianic secret

Scholars have long debated why, after this
open confession of Peter, Jesus still tried to
keep his true identity a secret – the so-called
'Messianic secret'. He ordered his disciples
not to tell anyone about his Messiahship and
to keep the truth to themselves. The reason
seems to be that Jesus did not have a problem
with being God's chosen Messiah, but only
with the general perception among the people
of what that meant. Even Peter did not really
understand what he was saying. He still had
in mind a military leader who would defeat
all of Israel's enemies – a far cry from the
suffering and dying figure that Jesus was
destined to be. It was a long time before the
disciples really understood and accepted that.

would come to earth to prepare the people for the coming of the Messiah.

The second question was, 'What about you… who do you say that I am?' Jesus invited his disciples to go much further and make their own judgment about him – not simply to repeat hearsay. On this

The Jews gathered around him, saying, 'How long will you keep us in suspense? If you are the Christ [the Messiah], tell us plainly.' Jesus answered, 'I did tell you, but you do not believe.'

JOHN 10:24–25

The town of Caesarea Philippi stood on a site that, in Old Testament times, had been a centre for Baal worship. During the Greek occupation the niches in this wall contained images of the god Pan. It was among all this religious confusion that Jesus chose to ask his disciples, 'Who do you say that I am?'

occasion, as on many others in the Gospels, Peter acted as the spokesman for the others: 'You are the Messiah.' This clearly indicated that Jesus was believed to be God's messenger who would restore the fortunes of Israel and its supremacy in the world. It was the first time that anyone had made such an open and unequivocal statement of belief in his mission.

There is a clear impression in all the Synoptic Gospels that from this moment onwards events moved very rapidly towards their conclusion in Jerusalem.

The Transfiguration

The transfiguration of Jesus is one of the most mysterious incidents in the Gospels. For a brief moment the event draws aside the curtain separating heaven and earth and the disciples glimpse his true nature as the Son of God.

The episode in which Jesus is 'transfigured' in front of his disciples is recorded in each of the Synoptic Gospels and follows closely on Peter's confession of faith in Jesus.

The three disciples

Peter, James and John formed an inner circle among Jesus' disciples, often called by Jesus to share his most intimate moments with him. They were present, for instance, when Jesus restored a dead girl to life and later when Jesus prayed in agony of spirit in the Garden of Gethsemane. For his transfiguration Jesus took them with him onto the lower reaches of Mount Hermon, a snow-capped mountain on Israel's northern border.

The cloud

Matthew's Jewish readers were familiar with their own scriptures and knew that their great ancestor, Moses, had been summoned by God to meet with him on a mountain to receive the precious Torah. As Moses climbed upwards a cloud covered him for six days and on the seventh day God spoke to him out of the cloud. In the Old Testament very few people were privileged to speak with God and no one ever saw God directly. A cloud always covered the divine glory.

Mount Hermon in northern Galilee, thought by some to be the site of Jesus' transfiguration.

The glory of Jesus

While they were on the mountain with Jesus the three disciples saw him change completely. The 'dazzling white' appearance he assumed was always associated in the Bible with angels and other divine beings. For a brief moment they saw Jesus as he really was, the Son of God, talking with the two most important Jewish religious leaders of the past: Moses, representing the Law, and Elijah, representing the Prophets. These two leaders summed up all that was important in Jewish religion.

The disciples were speechless but Peter, breaking the silence, offered to build shelters (tabernacles) for Jesus, Moses and Elijah. This would seem to indicate that the transfiguration took place during the Festival of Tabernacles, when Jewish families built their own shelters with leaves and branches in their homes to remind

I've been to the mountain top. And I've looked over, and I've seen the Promised Land... I'm not fearing any man. Mine eyes have seen the glory of the coming of the Lord.

MARTIN LUTHER KING, JR (1929–68), AFRICAN-AMERICAN CIVIL RIGHTS LEADER

themselves of the slavery their ancestors had left behind in Egypt. While Peter was speaking a voice from heaven spoke to all of them: 'This is my Son, whom I love; with him I am well pleased. Listen to him.' These words are almost identical to those which Jesus heard at his baptism. When they looked up again the disciples were alone with Jesus on the mountain.

The transfigured Jesus stands between Moses and Elijah, while his three closest disciples fall to the ground in fear at the sound of God's voice. *The Transfiguration of Our Lord*, 14th-century Russian icon.

Predicting Death

Jesus clearly knew at an early stage that he would be arrested, face judgment and be put to death in Jerusalem.

On three separate occasions Jesus tried to warn his disciples of his impending death, but each time they failed to grasp the meaning of what he said to them.

First warning

The first warning comes just after the turning point in Mark's Gospel, and in the life of Jesus, when Peter identified Jesus as God's Messiah. Jesus takes the opportunity to warn his disciples that 'the Son of man must suffer many things and be rejected by the elders, chief priests and teachers of the law, and that he must be killed and after three days rise again'.

These words were too much for Peter and he began to rebuke Jesus. In reply Jesus used the strongest possible language by identifying Peter with Satan because he had acted as if there was an easy way to fulfil God's will. Any remaining doubts that Jesus entertained about that will

Mary of Bethany anointed Jesus' feet with expensive perfume. Some around him were indignant about the waste of money, but Jesus saw in her action a prophetic reference to his death. 'Leave her alone!' he said. 'She poured perfume on my body to prepare it ahead of time for burial.' *Jesus Christ at Supper with Simon the Pharisee* (1072, Byzantine fresco) in Basilica San Angelo in Formis, Capua, Italy.

were to be overcome later in the Garden of Gethsemane.

Second warning

On a second occasion Jesus repeated his warning that he would be put to death and return to life three days later. Jesus taught that the kingdom of God belonged to those who were powerless – as he himself was now powerless to affect the tide of events – and insisted that it is for those without any power of their own that the Son of man had come to suffer and die.

Third warning

Towards the end of his life Jesus knew that he must reach the city of Jerusalem quickly. Taking his

We are going up to Jerusalem where the Son of man will be handed over to the chief priests and teachers of the law. They will condemn him to death and then hand him over to the Gentiles, who will mock him, spit on him, whip him, and kill him; but three days later he will rise to life.

MARK 10:33–34

disciples to one side he told them that once they arrived the Son of man would be handed over to the chief priest and teachers of the law. They in turn would hand him over to the Romans, who would mock him, spit on him and flog him. The Son of man would be killed by his enemies but, three days later, he would return to life.

A FAILURE TO UNDERSTAND

These warnings are very direct, but we have no way of knowing whether Mark was reporting the actual words of Jesus. He was writing more than 30 years after the event and his account is certainly coloured by what had happened in the meantime. Even so, the failure of the disciples to understand Jesus is puzzling. Jesus had made many enemies in his short ministry and it was common knowledge that they were plotting to kill him. It seems that the disciples deliberately shut their minds to the inescapable truth: the life of Jesus was going to be prematurely ended in a violent way.

In Jerusalem

Jesus' final journey to Jerusalem was marked by an increasing sense of gravity as he placed greater emphasis on the demands of discipleship and the conditions for entry into the kingdom of God.

Arriving at the Mount of Olives with his disciples, Jesus arranged his own entry into the city of Jerusalem. The journey was marked by an outbreak of popular nationalistic fervour which, quite naturally, set alarm bells ringing for the political and religious authorities. Their plot to bring about his downfall hints that the noisy popularity of Jesus was going to be short-lived. To the Gospel-writers, however, the arrival of Jesus riding on a donkey recalled an old prophecy and underlined the significance of the event: Jesus as the King of Peace in the city of God. The stress upon the humility of his arrival underscored the true nature of his kingship.

Cleansing the Temple

The first Temple in Jerusalem had been built by Solomon in the 10th century BCE but this was destroyed in 586 BCE. The present building had been started by the much-hated

> *God is the judge of all social systems.*
>
> OSCAR ROMERO (1917–80), ROMAN CATHOLIC ARCHBISHOP OF EL SALVADOR, MURDERED WHILE PREACHING

Herod the Great and the area cleansed by Jesus was the outer Court of the Gentiles, the only part of the Temple complex open to both Jews and non-Jews. This area of the Temple was used for two main activities: to sell animals for sacrifice in the Temple precincts and to change money. Roman money, carrying the head of the emperor, was never used in the Temple since it reminded the Jews that they were a subject people. Instead, Roman coins had to be changed for the old Hebrew coinage and the cost of doing this was very high. It was this that Jesus objected to so strongly.

Jesus overturned the tables of the money-changers and by doing this in the Court of the Gentiles he reminded people

Jesus rode into Jerusalem on a donkey to the acclaim of the crowds. But, as he came into view of the city, he wept over Jerusalem's failure to recognize God's salvation. *The Road to Jerusalem* by Fra Angelico (c. 1387–1455).

that God cared deeply for the welfare of everyone, Jews and Gentiles alike. This is the only occasion in the Gospels where Jesus used physical violence; although he used 'verbal violence' on more than one occasion, usually against the religious authorities. The spiritual significance of overturning the tables would not have been lost on the religious authorities. They knew only too well that cleansing the Temple, the house of God, was one of the first actions that the Messiah was expected to perform when he arrived. Once again Jesus was making it clear, by his actions, just who he was.

The Last Supper

Jesus ate one last meal, a Passover meal, with his disciples just before his arrest. He lent this meal special spiritual significance by using the bread and wine on the table to symbolize his forthcoming death.

At the last meal that Jesus ate with his disciples he told them that he did not expect to eat another meal with them on earth since his death was imminent. He took the opportunity to warn them that one of their number, Judas Iscariot, would betray him to the religious authorities. It was also at this meal that Jesus took a bowl of water and washed the feet of his disciples to show them the meaning of true humility – a necessary spiritual quality for those with ambitions to enter the kingdom of God.

The Passover meal

The symbolic significance of food was very much a part of the Passover ritual and so the disciples would not have been surprised that Jesus wanted to share this meal with them. They would, however, have been startled when he linked the bread and wine on the table with his forthcoming death.

Jesus took a loaf of bread, broke it, gave thanks and

The Last Supper was not a political event. It was a meal of redemption prepared by the compassionate God… The broken body of Jesus is different from ours. It is broken to release the redemptive power of God. Its blood is shed to give rise to a community of wholeness. It is the reign of God that breaks out of that broken body of Jesus.

CHOAN-SENG SONG,
TAIWANESE THEOLOGIAN

THE LAST SUPPER AND THE PASSOVER

Although we cannot be certain, it seems likely that Jesus was sharing this last meal with his disciples on the eve of the Passover festival. There was no more important festival in Judaism. It looked back to the great deliverance of the Jews from slavery and forward to the time when God would send the Messiah to set up his kingdom on earth. In fact, the Last Supper looked even further forward to the Messianic banquet which would mark the end of time, when Jesus would return to be accepted by all as their king.

The Passover meal that Jesus ate with his disciples immediately prior to his arrest has become known as the Last Supper. *Last Supper* (mural) in a church at Goreme, Turkey.

distributed it to his disciples. He had done exactly the same thing when he had miraculously fed a large crowd on just five loaves and some fish. Jesus told them that the bread represented his own body, which was shortly to be broken for them and the whole world on the cross.

Wine, diluted by water, was the common drink at all Jewish meals. At these meals God was always thanked for the fruit of the vine, but Jesus told his disciples that the wine in the goblet represented his blood which was going to be poured out on the cross for the salvation of many people.

As Jesus spoke to them his disciples would have recognized the allusion to the suffering servant of whom Isaiah the prophet had spoken centuries before. Jesus was telling them that he *was* the Messiah, but a Messiah who would suffer and die for the sins of others.

Gethsemane and Betrayal

Events in the life of Jesus moved swiftly towards their climax after the Last Supper. The key figure in the arrest of Jesus was Judas Iscariot, one of his disciples, who handed him over to the political and religious authorities.

After eating the Passover meal and singing a hymn Jesus and his disciples crossed the Kidron valley to the Mount of Olives, heading for a garden called Gethsemane (meaning 'wine-press'). Before reaching it Jesus warned his disciples that

crowed in the morning he would deny Jesus three times.

Gethsemane

Taking his three closest friends – Peter, James and John – with him, Jesus entered the Garden of Gethsemane to pray. The events

The moment of Jesus' arrest as Judas leads a group of soldiers to him, identifying Jesus by giving him a kiss. *The Betrayal of Jesus* (detail from the *Maestà* altarpiece) by Duccio di Buoninsegna (c. 1255–c. 1318).

all of them would desert him before the night was out. Typically, Peter protested his eternal loyalty but Jesus told him that before the cock

which followed highlighted the humanity and fragility of Jesus. Throughout the long hours of the night he struggled alone with God and with himself as he

While he was still speaking a crowd came up, and the man who was called Judas, one of the Twelve, was leading them. He approached Jesus to kiss him, but Jesus asked him, 'Judas, are you betraying the Son of man with a kiss?'

LUKE 22:47–48

disciples, found them sleeping, woke them up and admonished them. Jesus felt totally friendless. Finally, he returned to his disciples a third time, told them, 'It is enough,' and looked up to see Judas Iscariot leading a motley band of Temple guards, Roman soldiers and religious leaders coming to arrest him.

dreaded the immediate future. This agony of spirit is described vividly by all the Gospel-writers, but especially by Luke.

Jesus pleaded with God that the burden of what lay ahead might be lifted from him. Graphically we are told that beads of sweat, like great drops of blood, fell from his brow. Twice he returned to his

JUDAS ISCARIOT

His betrayal by Judas Iscariot did not take Jesus by surprise – he had anticipated it at the Last Supper. There is, however, no obvious motive for the betrayal. The money that Judas was paid – 30 pieces of silver – was a reasonable sum, but hardly enough in itself to persuade someone to betray a close friend. Perhaps Judas was expressing his disillusionment with Jesus and his way of nonviolence. He may even have been trying, as a last desperate throw of the dice, to force Jesus into taking decisive action against the Romans.

The arrest of Jesus

Judas singled Jesus out with the prearranged signal of a kiss. As Jesus was seized by the soldiers one of his disciples cut off the ear of the High Priest's servant. When he saw what had happened Jesus turned to his disciples and ordered that no further resistance be offered, since nothing must be allowed to stand in the way of God's will, which Jesus had struggled finally to accept in the Garden of Gethsemane. After healing the High Priest's servant Jesus reprimanded the crowd that had come out to arrest him with swords and clubs, as if he were no better than a common criminal. The way of violence, he stressed, was not his way and never had been.

Jesus offered no resistance when he was arrested, and made little attempt to defend himself in the trials that followed. By this time he was clearly reconciled to his death, because he believed it was an integral part of God's plan for the salvation of humanity.

There is abundant evidence from Roman, Jewish and Christian sources that Jesus' death was by crucifixion. Jews reacted strongly against this idea, basing their disgust on a passage from the Old Testament which stated that anyone crucified was cursed by God.

The Gospel-writers agree that God brought Jesus back from the dead. Jesus

Calvary (c. 1457–60) by Andrea Mantegna (c. 1431–1506).

then commissioned his followers to spread the good news, or gospel, throughout the world. The Gospels report that Jesus appeared to his disciples, and many of his followers, more than once during the 40 days after his resurrection, before finally ascending into heaven.

If a man guilty of a capital offence is put to death and his body is hung on a tree, you must not leave his body on the tree overnight. Be sure to bury him that same day, because anyone who is hung on a tree is under God's curse.

DEUTERONOMY 21:22–23

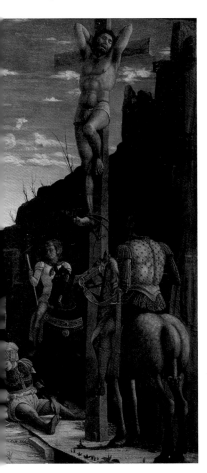

DEATH AND BEYOND

Contents

On Trial

Jesus faced two main trials, the first before the supreme
Jewish Council, the Sanhedrin, and the second in front
of Pontius Pilate, the Roman governor of Judea.

According to John, Jesus was
taken after his arrest before
Annas, a former High Priest,
who was still very powerful in
Jerusalem, before being sent on
to Caiaphas, the present holder
of the post and Annas' son-in-
law. It was during this time that
Peter joined the crowd to see
what was happening and, when

challenged, denied knowing Jesus
three times. Jesus, meanwhile,
in not defending himself when
accused, was showing that he did
not recognize the authority of
the Jewish leaders to try him.

Before the Sanhedrin

According to its own rules the
Sanhedrin had to find two

According to
Mark, Jesus was
tried at night
before the High
Priest and the
Sanhedrin.
However, the
known rules of
the Sanhedrin did
not allow trials to
be held at night.
Luke tells us that
the trial before
the Sanhedrin
took place at
daybreak.

Pontius Pilate
recognized that
it was the envy
of the Jewish
religious leaders
that motivated
them to demand
Christ's death.
*Jesus Before
Caiaphas* by
Giotto di
Bondone
(c. 1267–1337).

independent witnesses for any serious charge and their evidence had to be identical when they were out of earshot of each other. The witnesses could not agree on their evidence against Jesus. Some of them testified that Jesus had said that the Temple would be destroyed and rebuilt within three days. When Jesus agreed that he saw himself as the Messiah the High Priest tore his clothes in front of everyone – a traditional response to blasphemy. In Jewish eyes this 'crime' was worthy of death and the Sanhedrin unanimously condemned Jesus.

John's Gospel portrays Pontius Pilate, the Roman governor, as being unsettled by Jesus' presence and wanting to release him. But the Jews needed Pilate's approval before they could put Jesus to death. When they insisted that Jesus was challenging Caesar's authority by claiming to be a king, Pilate finally gave in and handed Jesus over to be crucified.

Before Pilate

By the time Jesus was taken before Pontius Pilate, the Roman governor of the province, the charge against him was changed from blasphemy – a religious charge of no interest to the Romans – to that of sedition, representing a threat to the stability of the Roman empire. The common perception of the Messiah figure was that of a

> *What is truth? said jesting Pilate and would not stay for an answer.*
>
> FRANCIS BACON (1561–1626),
> ENGLISH PHILOSOPHER
> AND ESSAYIST

political agitator who would challenge the power and authority of the emperor in Rome and, not surprisingly, this charge greatly concerned Pilate.

Pilate, it appears, was reluctant to condemn Jesus, although this is not in keeping with what is known of his character from contemporary sources which portray him very differently. Pilate tried to invoke a tradition which allowed the Roman authorities to release one prisoner chosen by the Jewish people each year before the festival of Passover began. Under this arrangement Pilate offered to release Jesus but, according to Mark, the offer was firmly rejected by the crowd under incitement from the priests and elders. The people chose Barabbas, a common criminal and murderer, instead of Jesus. Barabbas was released and Jesus condemned.

To the Cross

On his journey from the judgment hall of Pilate to his place of execution Jesus trod the well-worn path in Jerusalem which is now called the Via Dolorosa.

After the sentence of death was passed by Pilate Jesus was flogged and mocked before his execution – the normal practice in Roman-controlled Palestine. The soldiers' mockery held symbolic significance in Jesus' case: before the Sanhedrin Jesus had been accused of claiming to be a king; now, before the soldiers, he was mockingly treated as one. They dressed him in the imperial colour of purple and pressed a crown of thorns upon his head, to parody the crown of laurels worn by the emperor, while offering him their taunting homage. But the Gospel-writers set the record straight: Jesus, not the Roman emperor, was the real king of the world.

> *No trace is left in human or divine memory of those who inflicted the cross on others. Only those are remembered who carried a cross for the sake of others.*
>
> LEONARDO BOFF, BRAZILIAN LIBERATION THEOLOGIAN

The way to crucifixion

Normally, after the sentence of death was passed, the condemned man carried part of his cross on the steep uphill journey to the place of execution. Jesus started to do

There are mixed emotions from the crowd as Jesus carries his cross to Calvary. A religious leader drags him with determination, while the women of Jerusalem mourn for him. For the expressionless soldiers, it is just another day's work. *Road to Calvary* by Simone Martini (1284–1344).

THE WOMEN OF JERUSALEM

Luke tells us that there were many women who followed Jesus on his way to crucifixion; in keeping with Jewish custom they 'were beating their breasts and wailing for him'. These actions were normally reserved until after a person had died. Jesus addressed them as 'daughters of Jerusalem' and told them not to weep for him but for themselves and for their children. All of the Synoptic Gospels mention the presence at the crucifixion of women who had looked after Jesus in Galilee. Jesus was deserted by his disciples but his women followers remained faithful to the end.

It is not possible to be certain, but it seems likely that Jesus was crucified on 14 Nisan: 7 April 30 CE.

this but because of his weakened condition the burden proved too great. Instead a bystander, Simon from Cyrene in North Africa, was forced into carrying the cross for most of the way. Luke informs us that Simon carried the cross 'behind' Jesus, unconsciously illustrating Jesus' words about the need for a true disciple to take up his cross and follow him.

This is one of the events

represented in all Catholic churches in the 14 stations of the cross. Each Good Friday worshippers 'follow' in Jesus' footsteps up the Via Dolorosa (the 'Way of Sorrows') to Golgotha (the 'Place of the Skull'), where he was crucified. This journey is also commemorated weekly in Jerusalem as pilgrims and visitors to the city walk behind a wooden cross, stopping at each of the 14 stations marking places where Jesus is thought to have paused or stumbled on his way to execution.

John's Gospel assumes that Jesus was crucified 'outside the city walls' of Jerusalem, since this was in accordance with both Roman and Jewish law. The traditional site of the crucifixion, Golgotha or Calvary, was first identified in the fourth century and the Church of the Holy Sepulchre was built on the spot. No one, however, is completely sure about the true location of Golgotha.

Crucifixion

Jesus died remarkably quickly on the cross, no doubt weakened by the brutal treatment he had already received.

Crucified criminals were normally hung naked on the cross and exposed to the full ridicule of their fellow human beings but, because of their modesty about the human body, Jewish prisoners were allowed to wear a loin-cloth. The shape of the cross varied from place to place in the Roman empire: sometimes it was just an upright stake, sometimes X-shaped and often T-shaped. Traditionally, the cross on which Jesus died is an upright pole with a cross bar, to which he was nailed through

The Old Testament prophet Isaiah's words about Jesus are graphically illustrated in this painting: 'He had no beauty or majesty to attract us to him, nothing in his appearance that we should desire him. He was despised and rejected by men, a man of sorrows, and familiar with suffering.' *Head of Christ Crucified* by the Master of Liesborn (active during second half of 15th century).

The Gospels record the seven utterances that Jesus made from the cross, known as the Seven Last Words. They can be found in Mark 15:34, Luke 23:34, Luke 23:43, Luke 23:46, John 19:26–27, John 19:28 and John 19:30. These are treasured by many Christians.

both hands and feet. A small ledge under the feet allowed the prisoner to relieve the pressure of the body's weight on the arms.

The death of Jesus

According to Mark's timing the crucifixion began at 9.00 a.m. A notice was fixed above Jesus' Jesus explaining the reason for his execution: 'The King of the Jews'. The sign, written by Pilate, could have been intended as a statement of fact, an incitement designed to enrage the Jews or an ironic comment by the Roman governor on the impotence of Jesus, a king hanging helplessly on a cross.

The Gospels tell us that

The cross is God at work. It is not only his rack, it is his active self, his extracting and unifying role.

PAUL CLAUDEL, FRENCH POET, ESSAYIST AND DRAMATIST

THE CROSS AS A SYMBOL

Crucifixion was such a shameful way of dying that it was never used by the Jews, as a symbol of their resistance to the Romans. Yet, in the New Testament, the death of Jesus on the cross is not seen as a disgrace; instead it is interpreted by Paul and others as 'an at-one-ment', a way of reconciling a holy God with sinful humanity. This understanding of the death of Jesus is at the heart of the Christian message of salvation.

Jesus was crucified between two criminals. They had probably been condemned because they had committed politically motivated crimes and so were perceived to be a threat to Rome. These two criminals threw insults at Jesus. In Luke's account one of them repented and sought Jesus' forgiveness, but there is no mention of this in Mark's description.

Death from crucifixion was usually a lengthy process, often taking more than 24 hours, but Jesus died with astonishing speed: it seems from the Synoptic Gospels that the whole process lasted just six hours. When he was asked for Jesus' body by a secret follower, Joseph of Arimathea, Pilate expressed real surprise that he was already dead. The only disciple mentioned as being with Jesus at the end is John; Jesus gave him the responsibility of being a surrogate son to his mother, Mary. Three women are also mentioned as being there – Mary Magdalene, another Mary and Salome – and these women were to play a very important part in the events that followed three days later.

Burial

The burial of Jesus in the borrowed tomb of Joseph of Arimathea was a very rushed affair, sandwiched between his death in the middle of the afternoon and the start of the Sabbath day at nightfall.

The normal Roman custom was to leave the body of a crucified man at its place of execution for days so that it could be picked over by vultures. The Jewish scriptures, however, stipulated that a hanged man should be buried on the day of death before nightfall. Sometimes an influential Jewish person could intervene by obtaining the body quickly and making their own arrangements for its burial. This is what happened in the case of Jesus. Joseph of Arimathea was a respected member of the Sanhedrin who may well have been, as both Matthew and John imply, a secret disciple of Jesus.

After death

John tells us in his Gospel that a Jewish delegation asked Pilate if the body of Jesus could be taken down from the cross quickly so that the sanctity of the Sabbath day would not be violated. This is a little strange, as rabbinic law clearly allowed the burial of a body on the holy day if the occasion demanded it. This delegation assumed that the three victims of crucifixion would still be alive and requested that their legs be broken to hasten death. Jesus was already dead, but to make certain a soldier plunged his spear into his side releasing a flow of blood and water – a event of profound spiritual symbolism for the early Christians.

John describes how Joseph and his companion, Nicodemus, embalmed the body of Jesus in keeping with Jewish tradition, but the Synoptic writers tell us that the corpse was wrapped in a shroud immediately prior to burial, implying that there was no time to anoint the body. This seems more likely since there are clear hints that the proximity of the Sabbath day prevented the carrying out of full burial rites. Certainly when the women arrived at the tomb

> *There's nothing pretty about death. Those who sentimentalize it, lie.*
>
> CATHERINE MARSHALL, NORTH AMERICAN RELIGIOUS WRITER

on the first Easter morning they were expecting to carry out these traditional rituals.

All of the Gospels agree that Joseph interred the body in a tomb that had not been used before. Matthew tells us that this tomb had been hewn out by Joseph for his own future use and that of his family. After the body of Jesus was placed inside, the entrance to the tomb was sealed by a large stone which was rolled across the front. The Gospel-writers add this detail to underline that the death of Jesus was totally genuine, and the forthcoming resurrection correspondingly miraculous.

Jesus' body is taken from the cross and hurriedly deposited in a tomb provided by Joseph of Arimathea. *The Lamentation Before the Tomb* by Rogier van der Weyden (c. 1399–1464).

Resurrection

The belief that Jesus died and rose again three days later stands at the very heart of the Christian faith. Without the resurrection, as Paul commented, the Christian faith would be worthless.

Each Gospel-writer presents his own highly individual account of the resurrection of Jesus and though many attempts have been made to reconcile the four accounts it has proved to be impossible. Despite this, they all have an underlying thematic pattern which shows that they all come from a common, well-established tradition in the early Church.

The resurrection of Jesus

The four Gospel-writers all agree on one central fact: on the third day after Jesus died, the tomb in which his body had been placed was empty. The Synoptic Gospels emphasize strongly that there could have been no confusion and that the tomb the disciples visited was

> *Hope is the unshakeable certainty in the realization of the promises of God in Jesus Christ, based on Jesus' life, death and resurrection.*
>
> TISSA BALASURIYA,
> SRI LANKAN THEOLOGIAN

the one in which the body had previously been laid. They also agree that it was the three women present at the death of Jesus who visited the tomb early on the Sunday morning only to find the stone rolled away from the entrance. The women went to the tomb because they were concerned that the full Jewish burial rites had not been carried out.

The Synoptic writers also agree that the women were

confronted at some time or other by one or more supernatural beings (angels) who told them that Jesus was no longer dead but alive. In both Matthew's Gospel and Mark's Gospel the women were told to tell the disciples that Jesus was alive and that he was going ahead of them to Galilee,

Thomas missed the first appearance of the risen Jesus to his disciples, and refused to believe in his resurrection until he had seen Jesus with his own eyes. *The Incredulity of Saint Thomas* by Giovanni Battista Cima da Conegliano (c. 1459–c. 1518).

The entrance to a first-century tomb. After the body was placed inside, the stone would have been rolled in its channel across the entrance. Once it was in place, there was no possibility of anyone opening the grave from inside simply by pushing against the stone.

Gospel in some versions may have been added later. In both Matthew's Gospel and Luke's Gospel Jesus appears to his disciples and Matthew records the Great Commission by which Jesus charges his disciples with the responsibility for spreading his gospel message far and wide. Luke alone records the appearance of Jesus to two unnamed disciples making their way home from Jerusalem to Emmaus after the crucifixion. To begin with they do not recognize their companion but 'their eyes are opened' when he shares a meal with them and breaks bread in front of them. Jesus is also said to have appeared on an unspecified occasion to upwards of 500 disciples, although the Gospels do not record this.

where he would meet with his followers. Luke adds that Peter went to the tomb to verify the story of the women.

Appearances

Mark ends his Gospel strangely and very abruptly – we have the empty tomb and then nothing else. The ending attached to the

Ascension

The New Testament writers were convinced that the same Jesus who had been crucified and had risen from the dead was now seated 'on the right hand of God'. Only Luke describes the departure of Jesus from the earth.

In the opening verses of the Acts of the Apostles, Luke states that the risen Christ appeared many times to his disciples 'speaking about the kingdom of God'. On one occasion, while Jesus was eating with his disciples, Luke recalls, Jesus told them not to leave Jerusalem until they had been 'baptized' with the Holy Spirit. After Jesus had ascended into heaven 'two men dressed in white' stood by the disciples and promised them that Jesus would return in the same way as they had seen him go.

Luke's Gospel ends on the same note when Jesus blesses his disciples 'in the vicinity of Bethany' before being taken from them into heaven. The disciples, we are told, worshipped him as he left them, and then returned to

> It is not for you to know the times or dates the Father has set by his own authority. But you will receive power when the Holy Spirit comes on you; and you will be my witnesses in Jerusalem, and in all Judea and Samaria, and to the ends of the earth.
>
> ACTS 1:7–8

THE GREAT COMMISSION

Both Matthew and Luke record the final commission of Jesus to his disciples to make disciples from all nations, an instruction which authorized the Church to preach the gospel beyond the Jews to the Gentiles. People were to become disciples through a baptism administered 'in the name of the Father and of the Son and of the Holy Spirit', and this was to become the regular formula by which the Church carried out the sacrament. In John's Gospel Jesus also bestows on the Church the authority to forgive sins. The leadership of the Church fell, for a short time, on the shoulders of Peter, before it was taken up by Paul, the great apostle to the Gentiles.

historically, the event was clearly a prelude to the giving of the Holy Spirit to the disciples and, through them, to the whole Christian Church. This took place 50 days after the festival of Passover during another Jewish festival, the festival of Pentecost. Christians celebrate Pentecost today as the birthday of the Christian Church.

The ascension also marked the beginning of a new era – the era of the Holy Spirit. For a short time the incarnate Jesus had been with his followers on earth, but that time was now over. Jesus was still going to be with them but in another way. He had ascended into heaven but he remained with them through the Holy Spirit until the last days and the setting up of the Messianic kingdom on earth.

Just as Jesus' disciples were unprepared for his resurrection, so his ascension also took them by suprise. But they returned joyfully to Jerusalem, where they followed Jesus' instructions to remain there until the Holy Spirit came upon them. *The Ascension* from a Book of Hours, written for Cardinal Ascanio Maria Visconti Sforza, by the Master of the Arcimboldi Missal, Milan, c. 1500/1505.

Jerusalem with great joy, spending much time in the Temple praising God.

The meaning of the ascension

It is the meaning rather than the actual event of the ascension which carries such significance for Christians. Whatever actually happened

The Gospel-writers, the original interpreters of the life of Jesus, were not dispassionate biographers observing events from a distance, but committed believers writing about the one they knew to be the Son of God. This, combined with their Jewish background and lives as citizens of first-century Palestine, greatly influenced the picture of Jesus they bequeathed to us.

The Gospels were just the beginning of the work of trying to understand and interpret the life and teaching of Christ. Since then it has continued apace for two millennia through the work of writers, artists and others from hugely diverse backgrounds. Like the writers of the original Gospels they, too, have looked at Jesus from their own cultural, religious and historical perspectives. It would have been impossible for them to have done otherwise. As a consequence they have often arrived at very different pictures of Jesus which they have then sought to share with

Jesus portrayed in heaven as the sacrificial lamb. *The Adoration of the Lamb* by Jan van Eyck (c. 1390–1441).

others in their chosen medium. Some have found themselves fascinated by the divine and eternal in Jesus, while others have been attracted to the humanity and fragility of the one who saw himself as the Son of man.

Our faith in the God of revelation cannot be lived and understood abstractly, in some atemporal fashion. It can only be lived through the warp and woof of the events that make up history.

JEAN-MARC ELA,
SOCIOLOGIST AND THEOLOGICAL
WRITER FROM CAMEROON

JESUS THROUGH HISTORY

Contents

Jesus and the Church

Jesus set out to lay the foundations of a 'new Israel', a new body that would replace the 'old Israel' which had rejected him as their Messiah. This new Israel would be built on his own teaching and that of his apostles.

The Church is the living embodiment of the life and teaching of Jesus. There are many scholars, however, who doubt whether Jesus intended to found a Church, since there is little in his teaching to suggest that Jesus ever had this in mind. Instead, they claim, the Church was a kind of afterthought: Jesus believed that the world was going to end shortly after his death and the Church only came into existence when this did not happen.

A new Israel

From the writings of Paul and others in the decades after the death of Jesus it is clear that the first Christians saw themselves as inheritors of the expectations that God originally had in mind for the nation of Israel, the Chosen People. This is supported by the fact that Jesus chose 12 disciples, which would have suggested to people at the time a continuing link between them and the 12 tribes of Israel on which the nation was built.

Choosing 12 disciples suggests that Jesus believed that Israel would not accept him as their Messiah and so he was already looking to the future by

THE CHURCH AND COMMUNION

The earliest witness that we have in the New Testament to the Church's celebration of Communion is not the Gospels but Paul. To Paul this sacrament was an expression of that unity which drew all Christian believers into one body, the body of Christ, the Church. Communion looked forward to the Lord's return to earth and was to be enjoyed, until this happened, as an act of remembrance for the whole Church.

> Whenever you eat this bread and drink this cup, you proclaim the Lord's death until he comes.
>
> 1 CORINTHIANS 11:26

beginning to build up the 'new Israel', the Church. Jesus united the present and the future in his teaching about the kingdom of God, which provided the world. He pictured himself in his parables as the landowner who went away leaving his servants in charge of his home in his absence. The servants did not

The Church was born with the arrival of the Holy Spirit on the Day of Pentecost. A group of frightened disciples was transformed into the core of a dynamic movement that was to sweep through the Roman world. *The Coming of the Holy Ghost* from *Scenes from the Life of Christ and Psalter*, English, c. 1200.

spiritual foundation on which the Church was built.

Jesus made it clear that he expected the world to end but did not know when this would happen. He foresaw a community of people, united by their faith in him, which would be in a state of constant readiness for the end of the

know when their master would return but they knew that he expected them to be constantly looking out for him. This is what Jesus expected of his followers, the Church, until he returned.

Jesus in the Catacombs

The earliest forms of Christian art are those which are found in the catacombs beneath Rome. Many symbolic representations of Christ are scratched on the walls of these catacombs, including that of the fish, the vine and the lamb.

The Roman persecutions of the early Church from the mid-first century to the early fourth century were the first great test of the Church's ability to withstand intense pressure. To provide some degree of security a vast network of underground passages – the catacombs – were dug beneath the city of Rome to bury the many Christian dead. The passages were also safe meeting-places where believers gathered to preach the gospel and celebrate the Eucharist, or Lord's Supper, in safety.

Images of Jesus

Art was used in the catacombs as a way of instructing, inspiring and giving hope. Christians needed to be reassured about the basic beliefs that drew them to a Christian faith in the first place, particularly that death was not the end but only the beginning.

Wall-paintings were scattered all around the catacombs, with

In the relative safety of the labyrinthine passages and rooms beneath Rome, early believers celebrated the Lord's Supper. *Eucharistic Banquet* in the Greek Chapel, catacomb of St Priscilla, Rome.

*Everything [in the catacombs]
is so dark that the words of
the prophet are most fulfilled:
'they descend alive into hell'.*

ST JEROME (331–420),
CHURCH FATHER

When the Roman
persecution of
the Christians
had ended it
is thought that
as many as six
million believers
had been buried
in 50 catacombs.

primitive figures and shapes
scratched on the walls. Standard
symbols for Jesus were widely
used:

◆ Fish were linked in Christian
minds with the miracle of the
five loaves and fishes and the
promise that Jesus would make
his disciples 'fishers of men'.
The letters of the Greek word
for fish, *icthus*, were taken to
stand for 'Jesus Christ, Son
of God, Saviour' and this sign
became a kind of Christian logo
carved everywhere on
gravestones, coffins and walls.
◆ The vine was a symbol taken
from John's Gospel of the union
between Jesus and his Church.
◆ The Lamb of God who
'takes away the sins of the
world' was one of the favourite
images for Jesus.
◆ Another very popular early
Christian motif was that of
the good shepherd, with Jesus
portrayed as the shepherd who
faithfully fed his flock.

Certain events from the
Gospels captivated the minds
of these early Christian artists,
as they are found time and time
again in the catacombs. They
include the visit of the wise
men to the infant Jesus, the
baptism of Jesus by John the
Baptist, the healing of the
paralysed man and of the
woman with a haemorrhage, the
conversation of Jesus with the
woman at the well in Samaria,
and the raising to life of
Lazarus.

One key theme is missing
from the catacombs and from
other early expressions of
Christian art. There are no
representations of the passion
of Christ – his sufferings and
death. Crucifixion was such a
degrading punishment that it
took the Church centuries to
fully accept that Jesus had died
by this humiliating method of
execution. In fact, crucifixes as
part of Christian devotion did
not appear until after the end of
the first millennium, when the
cross became the most powerful
symbol of the Christian faith.

Artists and the Nativity

For centuries the Church was, more or less, the sole sponsor of art with the consequence that artistic expression and Christian worship were closely intertwined. While artists over the centuries have drawn freely from the whole life of Jesus they have found much inspiration in the birth of God in a Bethlehem stable (the nativity).

From the early examples of Christian art left behind in the catacombs of Rome onwards, drawings and paintings have been used as visual aids to help believers reach a deeper understanding of their faith.

For centuries the Church was almost the only patron of art and artists. This lasted until the Renaissance and the development of the idea of true human potential without the need for the support of religious faith. The Reformation split the Church into many denominations, so breaking the monopoly of the Catholic Church on religious faith. In the 19th century the scientific revolution made it increasingly difficult for people to believe in religious mystery. As a result the Church and the artist drifted apart.

The fact remains that many of the world's greatest works of art have a Christian theme and many of these are based on the two important events in the life of Jesus – his nativity and his death on the cross.

The nativity

Paintings of the nativity of Jesus have usually been symbolic and mystical in tone. By the fifth century the main elements of the traditional nativity – baby in a manger, Mary, Joseph and the animals (ox and ass) – were invariably present, shortly to be joined by the wise men, shepherds and angels to make up the nativity that we recognize today. The iconic tradition in Eastern Christianity found much early inspiration in highly stylized paintings of the Madonna and Child, while in the West they were already appearing together in paintings by the early medieval period. In icons the nativity was usually set in a

The nativity is a popular subject for artists. *The Adoration of the Shepherds* by Guido Reni (1575–1642).

dark cave rather than a stable, to symbolize the sinfulness of humanity.

Later paintings also reflected this union of

Painting can do for the illiterate what writing does for those who read.

ST GREGORY THE GREAT (c. 540–604), WRITER AND POPE

symbolism and mystery. Botticelli, in his work *Mystic Nativity*, brought together heaven and earth with angels holding hands on the stable roof and dancing around the golden entrance to heaven. Such mystical elements were largely lost when painting moved into a much more realistic phase with such works as Georges de la Tour's *The Adoration of the Shepherds*, painted more than a century later, in which a sturdy Mary stands by the manger with the visiting shepherds offering a lamb as a gift to the newborn – anticipating the role of Jesus as the paschal (Passover) lamb of sacrifice, an image linked with the Jewish Passover festival, during which lambs were ritually sacrificed to God.

Art and the Cross

The importance of the events at the close of Jesus' life to all Christian believers has been recognized by artists down the centuries. In the first few centuries of the Christian Church, however, artists were reluctant to paint the crucifixion, while the resurrection, by its very nature, has proved artistically challenging.

Artists through the ages have found a rich vein of inspiration in the Gospel events running from the Last Supper through to the death of Jesus on the cross and beyond to his resurrection from the tomb.

Painting the crucifixion

The earliest-known representations of the crucifixion of Jesus did not appear until the fifth or sixth centuries. From then onwards, and especially after the 13th century, every aspect of Christ's passion from the Last Supper and the arrest in the Garden of Gethsemane, through the trials before the Jewish and Roman authorities, to the suffering and death of Jesus on the cross was explored. In particular, artists

> *He who scorns painting loves neither philosophy nor nature.*
>
> LEONARDO DA VINCI (1452–1519), ITALIAN ARTIST AND ENGINEER

ART AND THE RESURRECTION

The resurrection of Jesus has also fascinated artists although, unlike the crucifixion, the event does not lend itself so readily to a realistic approach. Apart from the empty tomb, artists have often concentrated on other aspects. Caravaggio's *The Supper at Emmaus*, for example, beautifully captures the moment of revelation when the two disciples realize that it is the risen Jesus who is sharing a meal with them. Stanley Spencer's 20th-century masterpiece *The Resurrection, Cookham* contains many of the eccentricities associated with his work, including friends and family climbing out of graves to be welcomed by the risen Christ, who is standing by the church doorway in the village of Cookham, England, where the artist lived.

sought to enliven the passion of Christ by emphasizing his humanity.

At the same time a great deal of symbolism was introduced to show that the death of Jesus was not that of an ordinary human being. For example, in the 16th century Tintoretto painted many scenes

20th-century *Calvary* is striking in its simplicity. This series of four panels depicts Christ and the two criminals with whom he was crucified, their pale figures stark against the colourful background. Yet hope is apparent once again, this time in the form of a star above Christ's head.

Despite the crowd at the foot of the cross, Jesus was alone in his sufferings. *The Crucifixion* by Jacopo Tintoretto (1518–94).

from the crucifixion, including *The Crucifixion*, in which the scene is action-packed yet intensely moving. The central figure of Christ is a symbol of hope amid the surrounding darkness and chaos. By contrast, Craigie Aitchison's

Jesus and Women

The misogyny displayed throughout the Church's long history cannot be traced back to the ministry of Jesus. That ministry was characterized by an openness to all people, whether male or female, without distinction.

There were no women among the 12 disciples of Jesus but there were clearly many women who followed Jesus closely. Mary Magdalene, Joanna and Susanna are mentioned in Luke's Gospel, along with 'many others', as accompanying Jesus and his disciples on their travels. Significantly, Luke adds, they 'were helping to support them out of their own means'. Mark's Gospel reports that Mary Magdalene along with another Mary, the mother of James, and Salome were the first witnesses at the empty tomb on the resurrection morning.

*Christ was the only rabbi
who did not discriminate
against women in his time.*
GRACE ENEME,
PRESBYTERIAN FROM CAMEROON

Women were also prominent among those whom Jesus healed, including a 'daughter of Abraham' who had been disabled for 18 years, a woman whose constant haemorrhaging had led to her being a social outcast, and a Gentile woman whose daughter was demon-possessed. Jesus expressly stated that even the prostitutes were certain to enter God's kingdom ahead of those who relied on their own respectable but empty spirituality.

The Marys took note of the place where Jesus' corpse was laid, and returned immediately the Sabbath was over to give the body a proper anointing. To their amazement they were met by an angel who announced that Jesus had risen from the dead! *The Three Marys at the Sepulchre* by Annibale Carracci (1560–1609).

An assessment

Jesus clearly adopted a very positive attitude towards women and this marked him out as distinctive in such a male-dominated society. Often the spiritual attitude of the women around Jesus was in marked contrast to that of the men who were chosen to share his life with him. The disciples were slow to grasp what Jesus

was saying to them, but a woman who anointed Jesus' head was said to have anticipated his death, burial and resurrection. In the story of Mary and Martha recorded in Luke's Gospel, Mary was clearly the prototype of women in the early Church to whom full discipleship was extended from the beginning.

Jesus shocked his disciples by talking with a lone Samaritan woman. She had been excluded from her own community because of her immorality, but Jesus did not condemn her. *Christ and the woman of Samaria at the Well* from *Meditations on the Life of Christ*, Italian, 14th century.

Feminist scholarship has asked very difficult questions which the Church ignores at its peril. Not only does it question the desirability of using biblical examples in any discussion in the 21st century, but it also raises unanswered questions about masculinity, homosexuality and power and inequality – both within the Church and within contemporary society. In order to retain its credibility in the 21st century the Church needs, among other things, to face these fundamental issues.

Jesus and Judaism

Although Christianity started life as a sect within Judaism, relations between them soon became fraught and have remained so for 2,000 years. Anti-Semitism led to many of the most disgraceful episodes in the Church's history.

Jesus was a practising Jew and at no time did he suggest to his followers that they should leave the Jewish faith. He made it clear to them that he had been sent to preach God's good news to the Jews first and only after that to the Gentiles. In 51 CE Church leaders, including Peter and Paul, met in Jerusalem to decide whether new converts to the faith should follow any Jewish religious practices, as the Jewish Christians did. Although the outcome was a compromise the Jewish voice in the Church became increasingly marginalized from that moment onwards. The hope expressed by Paul that the Jewish rejection of Jesus would only be temporary was not realized.

Issues at stake

After a brief revolt by the Jews the city of Jerusalem was wiped out by the Romans in 70 CE

Anti-Semitism was prevalent under Christian rule in the 17th century, as this etching of an attack on the Frankfurt Jewry shows. *The Plunder of the Ghetto Following the Fettmilch Riots in August 1614*, engraved by H. Merian.

> *The greatest friend of Truth is Time, her greatest enemy is Prejudice, and her constant companion is Humility.*
>
> CHARLES CALEB COLTON
> (1780–1832), ENGLISH POET

During the medieval period sculptures on church buildings showed the contempt in which Christians held the Jews. The eyes on statues were blindfolded to show the blindness of the Jewish people, while a broken lance, one of the instruments of the crucifixion, was often placed in the Jewish figure's hand.

and the rift between Christianity and Judaism widened into a chasm. Christians were expelled from their local synagogues and many were taken before local Jewish tribunals. The blame for the death of Jesus was shifted noticeably from Pontius Pilate to the Jewish people as a whole. In the days following the gift of the Holy Spirit at Pentecost Peter had blamed Jewish ignorance for their failure to welcome Jesus as their Messiah, but now there was a hardening of attitudes. This is clearly seen in John's Gospel where the Jews and Jesus are set on a collision course from the very outset of his ministry.

Anti-Judaism became a prominent feature of Christian evangelism throughout the Roman period, the Crusades and the Reformation. During the 19th century it developed into its most frightful expression – anti-Semitism – and this reached its zenith in the Nazi Holocaust. During the Holocaust more than six million Jewish men, women and children were killed by the Nazis.

The Talmud

The Talmud is the most authoritative repository of Jewish teaching apart from the scriptures themselves. The Talmud contains the statement that Jesus was hanged by the authorities because he committed sorcery in his attempt to lead Israel into apostasy – a departure from its true and revealed faith. No more serious charge can be laid against a Jew. The charge that Jesus had tried to lead Israel astray was, no doubt, prompted by the Church moving away from its strict adherence to the Torah to more of an 'open-door' policy towards the Gentiles.

Jesus and Islam

In Islam Jesus is given great respect as one of the prophets who prepared people for the coming of Muhammad, but Muslims do not believe that he was the divine Son of God, nor that he was crucified.

The Qur'an, the holy book of Islam, mentions 25 prophets by name of which five, including Isa (the Arabic name for Jesus), are 'major prophets'. These men were sent by God (Allah) to declare his word. This word was given to Moses (another of the major prophets), to declare to the Jews, and to Jesus, God's spokesman to the Christian community. Muslims have the greatest respect for both Jews and Christians because, like them, they are 'Peoples of the Book'. Muslims believe that Muhammad was the final and greatest of the prophets (the 'Seal of the Prophets') and that he was unique so can have no successor.

Jesus in the Qur'an

Many events in the life of Jesus are referred to in the Qur'an, although the details are often different from descriptions of the same events in the Gospels. For instance, John the Baptist is mentioned in the Qur'an, as are the virgin

There are unbelievers who say, 'God is the Third of Three'. No god is there but One God.

THE QUR'AN

birth, the annunciation to Mary and the birth of Jesus, which takes place under a date palm rather than in a stable. Mary shook dates from the tree for her baby to eat, while a stream of water flowed from its roots. Muslims accept that Jesus performed miracles but those recorded in the Qur'an owe more to fanciful stories found in the apocryphal Gospels (those of doubtful authenticity, such as the Gospel of Thomas, which is not actually included in the New Testament) than they do to those in the New Testament itself.

The teachings of Jesus

There are some clear echoes of the teaching of Jesus in the Qur'an. At least two of the parables are alluded to, as is the attitude of Jesus towards the Torah, the Jewish law. Several vital Christian beliefs are expressly denied, among them Christ's divinity. The idea that Allah could share his divinity with anyone is totally unacceptable to Muslims. They believe Muhammad was not divine and neither was Jesus. The Qur'an also denies that God is a Trinity. Muslims say that Jesus could not have died as a sacrifice to save us from our sins, since each person is held responsible by God for their own sinful actions. In fact, Muslims believe that Jesus was miraculously saved from death on the cross by a double who was put to death in his place. Jesus ascended directly into heaven from where he will return again at the end of the world.

It seems that Muhammad had little contact with the picture of Jesus presented in the four Gospels. Instead, his experience of Christianity was largely confined to wandering monks who brought a version of the faith heavily influenced by folklore and local traditions.

A miniature of the Angel Gabriel, who appears as a heavenly messenger in the Bible, and whom Muslims venerate as the revealer of the Qur'an

Jesus in Different Cultures

Over the centuries the Christian gospel has increasingly expressed itself in the cultural traditions of the people receiving it. People have also expressed their own Christian beliefs and worship in the same way.

Although the Christian gospel had extended well beyond the land of Palestine and the Mediterranean Sea by the 16th century, it was not until the early years of the 17th century that the great missionary expansion of the faith began. In 1719 Isaac Watts wrote a hymn which, more than any other, expresses confidence in the final triumph of Christianity.

Evangelization and imperialism

The expansion of Christianity was never simply a cloak for the spread of white imperialism, but it is a fact that alien ideas were often imported into traditional cultures through Christian evangelism, often with disastrous consequences. Early Jesuit work in China, for instance, under the leadership of Francis Xavier, had insisted on the traditional worship of the Mass with the compulsory use of Latin and the forbidding of any vernacular expression. By the late 16th century,

Paul, in his letter to the church at Philippi, describes Christ in glory with all the peoples and nations of the earth worshipping him.

Jesus shall reign where'er the sun
Does his successive journeys run;
His kingdom stretch from shore to shore,
Till moons shall wax and wane no more.
People and realms of every tongue
Dwell on his love with sweetest song.

ISAAC WATTS (1674–1748)

A 20th-century interpretation of the Last Supper in an African setting. *The Last Supper* by Elimo Njau.

first alphabets in numerous foreign languages.

Artistic expressions

As Christian worship began to take on more vernacular forms so did artistic expressions of Christian faith. For example, the black face of Jesus in works of art from the American black community and from Africa not only reflect the physical and cultural background of the artists, but also the fact that Jesus was certainly dark skinned, if not black, himself.

however, the Jesuit Matteo Ricci was wearing Buddhist clothes and had become a renowned scholar in all things Chinese.

Ricci remained an orthodox Catholic but saw clearly that the Christian gospel had to be expressed in ways that were not destructive of traditional cultures. A great step forward was taken in the 19th century when a number of Christian missions closely identified themselves with campaigns for literacy in many parts of the world. The desire to translate the scriptures into new tongues, a strong missionary imperative, often required the initial formulation of a language into a written form. Thus Christian missionaries produced the first dictionaries, wrote the first grammars and developed the

In an age where everyone has become aware of the ravages of hunger, disease, oppression and war two pictures of Jesus are particularly inspiring: Jesus the healer and Jesus the liberator. Jesus brought words of comfort together with acts of compassion and healing and this remains the mission of the Church. In many countries, especially in Latin America, the image of Jesus the liberator brings hope to the downtrodden, oppressed and persecuted.

149

Jesus in Film

Since the early 20th century the life of Jesus has been frequently depicted on screen. These portrayals have ranged from large-budget biblical epics to modest but more serious attempts to make statements of faith.

Since the early days of film, representations of Jesus have been controversial. Criticism came both from those who felt that any visual representation of Jesus was in bad taste, and from those who maintained that Jesus belonged in the Church, not the cinema.

Early films

Despite the controversy, the life of Jesus proved a magnet to early movie-makers. The first feature-length film on the subject was made in 1912, on location in Egypt and Palestine, and not only brought the Bible to life but enabled audiences to make a virtual pilgrimage to the Promised Land. Cecil B. Demille's largely silent *King of Kings* followed in 1927, in which Demille expressly exonerated the Jewish people for Jesus' death by pinning responsibility on one individual.

A new era

It was many years before another film tackled Jesus' life. Jesus had little more than a bit part in *Quo*

Jesus sits down to a meal with the Pharisees. A still from Franco Zeffirelli's *Jesus of Nazareth* (1977).

Vadis (1951), while his voice alone featured in *Salome* and *The Robe*, both of which came out in 1953. In the 1950s biblical blockbusters were all the rage, reaching a peak with *Ben Hur* (1959), in which there was no direct portrayal of Christ. *The Greatest Story Ever Told* (1965) cast an unknown actor as Christ and gave bit parts to many familiar Hollywood faces, but the film flopped.

New ground was broken in the 1960s by *The Gospel According to St Matthew* (1964). Its Italian director, Pier Paulo Pasolini, was the first to base a film entirely on a single Gospel; he chose Matthew because it conveyed the 'passionate violence of [Jesus'] politics'. In *Jesus Christ Superstar* (1973) Jesus was the enemy of the establishment, a man swept away by his own fame. In Franco Zeffirelli's *Jesus of Nazareth* (1977), which was made for television, the Jewish background of the story was portrayed very sympathetically, with Jesus taking on an otherworldly persona.

Monty Python's *Life of Brian* (1979) used vulgar and irreverent humour to send up both biblical epics and first-century Palestinian politics. The use of four-letter words and full-frontal nudity led to the film being banned in many places in Great Britain and across America, although it did not satirize Jesus, mocking instead the crowds that went looking for messiah figures all over early Palestine. The title refers to an ordinary man who is mistaken for a prophet.

Other controversial films followed *Life of Brian*, including Jean-Luc Godard's *Hail Mary* (1985) and Martin Scorsese's *The Last Temptation of Christ* (1988). Denys Arcand's *Jesus of Montreal* (1989) managed to avoid the fierce controversy of such films, partly perhaps because it openly acknowledged that it was primarily allegorical. Arcand draws a parallel between Daniel Coulombe, the actor who creates the passion play at the centre of the film, and Jesus of Nazareth. Like Jesus, Coulombe is surrounded by people who offer him worldly success, by admirers who spread misleading reports about his play and by irate authorities who want to shut him up. There is, though, little hope at the end of the film; instead Coulombe despairs that all human endeavours will prove transitory.

In recent years film-makers have taken fewer risks with Jesus. *The Miracle Maker* (2000) was the first film to tell the story of Jesus through animation, but the treatment of the story is largely conservative and uncontroversial.

Film-makers ought to have the opportunity to nudge viewers out of their comfortable, conventional ways of reciting the story of how God became man and lived among us; they can do this by portraying elements in the Gospels that previous films have suppressed, and by fleshing out those elements which the Gospels don't address. Audiences, meanwhile, need to respond to these films more cautiously, and to think about them more critically. If we don't, we run the risk of seeing but never perceiving, and hearing but never understanding.

PETER CHATTAWAY,
AMERICAN WRITER ON FILMS

Jesus Beyond the Church

While the institutional Churches decline in numbers and influence in the Western world, the person of Jesus Christ continues to attract and fascinate. For some, he has become an icon of popular culture amid the general disillusionment with the Church and organized religion.

Few people outside the Church are put off Christianity by the person and message of Jesus. In fact, the many who express disaffection with the Church as an institution frequently point to Jesus as someone to admire and respect. Why then this attraction to Jesus beyond the confines of the Church?

According to Harry Maier, a Lutheran pastor and professor of New Testament, Jesus lends himself very well to today's values. 'He's a pluralist, he welcomes outsiders, he welcomes women, he is against organized religion, he's for economic justice. Jesus comes dressed up in the clothes of our own culture.' This is the Jesus of the Jesus Seminar, a group of New Testament scholars who have become influential since they started meeting in the United States in 1985. They come together twice a year to discuss the historical accuracy of the words and deeds of Jesus as they have come down to us.

Jesus and the spiritual search

Jesus has become someone to identify with away from the demands of the Church. Focusing on the person of Jesus enables people to have a religious experience without any institutional tie-in. Allied to the growing interest in Jesus is the search for spirituality. Again, this does not result in more people going to church; rather, it means the popularity of retreats to monasteries, silent

> *Who was Jesus out to get? The thieves and the whores. He was looking to get the lowest of the low; he was looking to help the lepers to pray for themselves. They didn't need to go to these fancy scribes and Pharisees, and, like, bring a lamb or a gold shekel and say, 'Will you say a prayer for me?' He was saying, 'If you want to talk to God, you can talk for free: mention my name — you're in.'*
>
> PATTI SMITH,
> NORTH AMERICAN SINGER

prayer, spirituality seminars, an increasing number of books on spiritual paths, including Buddhist, Jungian and New Age (an umbrella term for a whole range of alternative spiritualities and therapies including tarot cards, crystals and paganism).

Questions such as 'What happens when we die?' are back in vogue and a rash of recent Hollywood movies – such as *Meet Joe Black*, *City of Angels*, and *What Dreams May Come* – ponder the afterlife. For many social commentators this is not a surprising development in the highly individual-orientated Western world: people are seeking a personal experience of God and want to 'pick and mix' what suits them best. They do not want what they perceive to be an authoritarian institution telling them what to do. In today's world Jesus is cool, the Church is not.

What is the attraction of Jesus outside the Church? Many people think Jesus has much to offer those seeking to make sense of the big questions of life. *Head of Christ* by Leonardo da Vinci, (1452–1519).

THE CHALLENGE TO THE CHURCH IN THE WEST

While some Christians have discounted 'pick-and-mix' spirituality as superficial and meaningless, others, such as the British theologian, John Drane are seeking to respond to the challenge. He writes,

The gap between Christian faith and the new spirituality is far wider than it needs to be. The people who search for meaning in neo-paganism, or the human potential movement, or through channeling or encounters with angels, are not monsters but, according to the very first page of the Bible, women and men made in God's image. They are seeking to discover how they can become most truly human, fulfilling their destiny within the cosmos, and will use whatever stories and methods seem to produce positive results. That, in essence, is what the teaching of Jesus is also about – so why do Christians find it so hard to relate to these people?

Drane and others like him are engaging in dialogue with today's spiritual seekers through, for example, literature and events such as psychic fairs. They are also urging Churches to respond to the questions such seekers ask.

Rapid Factfinder

A

Abraham: also known as Abram; lived about 1900 BCE around the Fertile Crescent area of Mesopotamia; came to believe in the one God and promised that descendants would be many and powerful; father of the Jewish nation.

Acts of the Apostles: fifth book of the New Testament; authorship traditionally linked to Luke who also wrote a Gospel; continues the story of the early Christians after Jesus left the earth.

Allah: God in the Islamic religion.

Andrew: brother of Simon Peter; he was fishing with his brother in the Sea of Galilee when Jesus called him to be a disciple.

Anna: elderly and devout Jewish prophetess who welcomed the infant Jesus in the Temple.

Annas: Jewish High Priest from 6 to 15 CE; father-in-law of Caiaphas, continued to hold an influential position after 15 CE; presided over the preliminary hearing of the case against Jesus.

anti-Semitism: hatred directed against Semitic people, has come to mean hatred directed specifically against the Jews for their Jewishness and role in the condemnation of Jesus.

Apocrypha: section in Protestant Bibles separate from the Old and New Testaments containing a number of later Jewish works, written in Greek rather than in Hebrew; 'deuterocanonical' books of secondary importance included in the Roman Catholic Old Testament.

apocryphal Gospels: Gospels not included in the New Testament canon due to being of doubtful authenticity, for example the Gospel of Thomas.

apostle: from the Greek meaning 'one who is sent'; name given to the disciples after the Day of Pentecost who were called to bear witness to the message of Jesus and to continue his work.

ascension: the rising of Jesus into heaven from earth 40 days after his resurrection; described in Luke's Gospel and in the Acts of the Apostles.

B

baptism: Greek for 'to dip in' or 'to wash'; rite of initiation used in Judaism and by John the Baptist (Jesus was baptized by John in the River Jordan); ancient Christian rite carried out on children and adults symbolizing rising to new life with Christ.

Barabbas: 'Son of the Father'; prisoner released in place of Jesus by Pontius Pilate.

Beatitudes: 'blessings'; part of Jesus' Sermon on the Mount where nine groups of people are said to be 'blessed' by God; spiritual characteristics to be shown by those who wish to be members of God's kingdom.

Bethlehem: small town about eight kilometres south of Jerusalem; birthplace of the Old Testament's King David; birthplace of Jesus.

Bible: sacred scriptures of the Christian Church; incorporates the Jewish scriptures with those held to be sacred by Christians; comprises the Old and New Testaments.

C

Caiaphas: son-in-law of and successor to Annas as High Priest in Jerusalem; in office from 18 to 37 CE; condemned Jesus before sending him to the Roman procurator.

Calvary: 'Place of the Skull'; 'Golgotha' in Aramaic; situated outside the city of Jerusalem; where Jesus was executed.

canonical Gospels: the four Gospels of Matthew, Mark, Luke and John, which are accepted as authoritative and included in the canon of scripture.

catacombs: extensive underground tunnels beneath the city of Rome; where early Christians buried their dead and held worship services away from the threat of Roman persecution.

Communion: Christian sacrament which commemorates the death of Jesus; also called the Lord's Supper in the New Testament.

Court of the Gentiles: one of four courts in Herod the Great's Temple; open to everyone whether Gentile or Jewish; the least exclusive court.

Court of the Israelites: place between the Holy of Holies and the Court of the Women in Herod's Temple; entry restricted to Jewish men.

Court of the Women: court in Herod's Temple between those of the Israelites and the Gentiles; its use was restricted to Jewish men and women; place where acts of worship were carried out but not sacrifices.

crucifix: model of Christ on the cross found in many Christian Churches; sometimes worn as a piece of jewellery.

crucifixion: method of execution used by the Romans throughout their empire; an exceedingly cruel and humiliating form of capital punishment. Because it was so cruel the Romans would not crucify any of their own citizens, but reserved the punishment for foreigners and slaves.

Crusades: wars fought from the 12th century by Christian armies organized by various Popes; directed against Muslims although Jews were often caught up in the bloodshed.

D

David: celebrated in the Old Testament as Israel's ideal king; celebrated in the New Testament as the ancestor of the Messiah; became king around 1000 BCE.

Day of Atonement: Yom Kippur; the most solemn day in the Jewish year; day of fasting on which Jews offer God repentance to atone for the sins they have committed in the previous 12 months; brings to an end the ten days of repentance which start on Rosh Hashanah.

Day of Pentecost: Jewish agricultural festival on which the Holy Spirit was given to the early Christians; festival held 40 days after Passover; marks the birthday of the Christian Church.

Dead Sea Scrolls: documents first unearthed accidentally in 1947 on the west side of the Dead Sea at Qumran including the oldest extant documents of many Old Testament passages and books; most important biblical archeological find of the 20th century.

disciple: 'pupil'; used in the Gospels to refer to 12 special friends chosen by Jesus to accompany him on his travels; applied to anyone who accepts the discipline of Jesus and commits themselves to him.

E

Elijah: most notable of the Old Testament prophets from the ninth century BCE; the Gospel-writers looked on John the Baptist as the new Elijah; represented the prophetic tradition in meeting with Jesus and Moses on Mount of Transfiguration.

Elisha: designated successor to Elijah; lived in the second half of the ninth century BCE; believed, like Elijah and Jesus, to have raised a widow's son from the dead.

Elizabeth: wife of the priest Zechariah; after years of infertility she gave birth to John the Baptist.

epistle: 'letter'; term applied to 21 books in the New Testament carrying such names as Paul, Peter and John; sent to individuals and church communities and much valued by the early Church.

Essenes: group within Palestinian Judaism existing from the second century BCE to 70 CE when Jerusalem was destroyed; not mentioned in Gospels but John the Baptist may have belonged to Essene community for a short time.

exodus: journey taken by the Israelites (Jews) in the 13th century BCE when God led them out of Egyptian slavery and into the Promised Land of Canaan.

exorcism: expulsion of evil spirits; some acts of exorcism are attributed to Jesus in the Gospels.

G

Gabriel: one of the chief archangels; appears in the Old Testament as a messenger from God; appears in the New Testament as herald of the supernatural births of John the Baptist and Jesus.

Galilee: northern part of Palestine; Nazareth and Capernaum were in Galilee; scene of early preaching and healing ministry of Jesus.

Garden of Gethsemane: 'oil-press'; located across the Kidron Valley on the western side of the Mount of Olives outside Jerusalem; place where Jesus prayed in agony before his arrest.

Gentile: everyone who is not a Jew.

Golgotha: Aramaic meaning 'Place of the Skull'; site for the execution of Jesus situated outside the walls of the city of Jerusalem.

Good Friday: day on which Christians worldwide remember

the crucifixion of Jesus; celebrated since the fourth century.

gospel: 'good news'; from the second century onwards applied to the four books of Matthew, Mark, Luke and John, which contain the 'good news' about Jesus.

H

Hanukkah: minor Jewish festival held to celebrate the rededication of the Temple by Judas Maccabeus in 164 BCE; also known as the Feast of Dedication.

hellenization: process by which many Jewish customs were affected by Greek culture in the two centuries before the Romans invaded Palestine.

Herod the Great: ruled Palestine as a surrogate for the Romans from 37 to 4 BCE; occupied the throne when Jesus was born; his territory was divided between his three sons on his death.

High Priest: occupied honoured place in Jewish religion, position filled by Annas and then Caiaphas during lifetime of Jesus, condemned Jesus after arrest before passing him over to Pontius Pilate.

Holocaust: murder of six million Jewish people by the Nazis during the Second World War.

Holy of Holies: inner sanctuary in Solomon's and Herod's Temples; the residence of God; only entered once a year by the High Priest on the Day of Atonement.

Holy Place: at the centre of Solomon's and Herod's Temples

adjacent to the Holy of Holies; held an altar, 10 golden lamp-stands and a table for the bread of the presence.

Holy Spirit: third member of the Christian Trinity; the power of God in the creation of the world; empowerer of Jesus; given to the Church on the Day of Pentecost.

Holy Week: Christian festival commemorating the last week in the life of Jesus; runs from Palm Sunday to Good Friday.

I

icon: visual representation of Jesus Christ, the Virgin Mary, the holy family or the saints; used as an aid to devotion in Eastern Orthodox Christianity.

incarnation: 'becoming flesh'; central mystery of the Christian faith whereby Jesus, who was God, became a human being.

Isaiah: son of Amoz; citizen of Jerusalem; adviser to four Israelite kings between 740 and 701 BCE; book named after him in the Old Testament contains some of the best-known prophecies about the coming of the Messiah.

J

Jacob: son of Isaac and Rebekah; lived sometime between 1750 and 1570 BCE; Jewish ancestor and patriarch.

James: son of Zebedee and brother of John; chosen by Jesus to be a disciple; formed an inner circle of disciples with Peter and John; became a leading light in the Jerusalem Church after the Day of Pentecost; stoned to death in 61 CE.

Jerusalem: key city in both the Old and New Testaments; at the heart of Islam, Judaism and Christianity; scene of the crucifixion of Jesus.

John: son of Zebedee and brother of James; became, with Peter and his brother, one of the group especially close to Jesus.

John the Baptist: cousin of Jesus; his preaching prepared the people for the coming of the Messiah; put to death by Herod.

Joseph: husband of Mary, mother of Jesus, and a descendant of King David; disappears from the Gospel narrative after the childhood of Jesus, so presumed to have died early.

Josephus: Jewish historian who lived between 37 and 95 CE; writer of *The Jewish War* and *Antiquities of the Jews*.

Judas Iscariot: one of the 12 disciples; name may come from the Greek for 'assassin'; betrayer of Jesus; there are two different accounts of his suicide in Matthew's Gospel and the Acts of the Apostles.

K

Ketuvim: the Writings; one of three divisions into which the Jewish scriptures are divided.

kingdom of God: 'rule' or 'kingship' of God; central theme of Jesus' teaching according to the Synoptic Gospels; brought near by Jesus but its final manifestation will be in the future.

kingdom of heaven: used by Matthew instead of 'kingdom of God', displaying the Jewish reluctance to use the name 'God'.

L

Last Supper: last meal Jesus shared with his disciples before his arrest, trial and crucifixion; inspiration behind the regular Christian celebration of Communion.

Lord's Prayer: given to the disciples at their request by Jesus; expresses hope that God will fulfil his purposes on earth as they have already been achieved in heaven.

Lord's Supper: Paul's name for the service held by early Christians to remember the Last Supper and the death of Jesus; used by some Churches to describe Communion today.

Luke: physician and companion of Paul; possibly the author of the Gospel that bears his name and the Acts of the Apostles.

M

Magnificat: Latin for 'magnifies'; first word of Mary's canticle or psalm expressing her joy at being chosen to be the mother of Jesus.

Mark: early companion of Peter; possibly the author of the Gospel written around 65 CE that bears his name and concentrates on the theme of the suffering Messiah.

Mary, mother of Jesus: gave birth to Jesus by the Holy Spirit in what is known as the virgin birth; known in the early Church as the Virgin Mary.

Mary Magdalene: leader of group of women who accompanied Jesus on many of his travels; healed by Jesus of a serious disease; gave the news of Jesus' resurrection to his disciples.

Mass: central Roman Catholic service of Communion.

Matthew: one of the 12 disciples; called to follow Jesus when he was sitting in his tax office; name attached to one of the Gospels.

Maundy Thursday: day in Christian year before Good Friday; commemorates the last meal that Jesus had with his disciples, during which he washed their feet and spoke about his forthcoming death.

Messiah: 'Anointed One' or 'Christ'; leader promised to the Jews in the Old Testament; title applied to Jesus by the early Church but only alluded to in the Gospels.

mezuzah: small leather container holding a parchment copy of the Jewish *Shema*; pinned to the doorpost of most rooms in the Jewish household; reminder of the basic statement of Jewish belief.

Moses: leader of the Israelites out of Egyptian slavery in the 13th century BCE; received the Ten Commandments from God on Mount Sinai; appeared with Elijah on the Mount of Transfiguration to represent the Old Testament Law.

Mount of Olives: hill about 1.6 kilometres to the east of Jerusalem on which Gethsemane was situated; Jesus visited it to pray.

Muhammad: Prophet of Islam born 570 CE; received divine revelations from Allah that are written in the Qur'an; died 632 CE.

Muslim: 'one who submits'; person who submits his or her life to Allah; follower of Islam.

N

Nazareth: town halfway between the Sea of Galilee and the Mediterranean Sea; residence of Mary and Joseph; place where Jesus lived until he became a public figure.

Nevi'im: the Prophets; one of three divisions into which the Jewish scriptures are divided.

New Testament: twenty-seven books comprising the Christian part of the Bible; contains the Gospels, the Acts of the Apostles, the epistles of Paul, Peter, John and others and the book of Revelation.

Nunc Dimittis: first words of the Latin canticle based on the words of Simeon when he held the infant Jesus; words used in some Churches.

O

Old Testament: the Jewish scriptures; the first part of the Christian Bible; 39 books of history, poetry and prophecy.

P

Palestine: the country within which most of the events in the Old and New Testaments took place, now known as Israel.

Palm Sunday: day on which Christians remember the triumphal entry of Jesus into Jerusalem on a donkey; first day of Holy Week.

Papias: second-century leader of a Christian community at Hierapolis in Asia Minor.

Parable: teaching by means of using a comparison; story containing a message over and above its literal meaning; a human story making a spiritual point.

paschal lamb: lamb sacrificed at Passover; Jesus.

Passion: the suffering, death and resurrection of Christ.

Passover: annual Jewish festival commemorating delivery of the Jews from Egyptian slavery and their journey to the Promised Land of Canaan.

Paul: convert to Christianity on the Damascus road; outstanding leader of the early Church; great missionary who established many churches around the Mediterranean Sea; writer of many letters (epistles) in the New Testament; died 64–66 CE.

Pentecost: the Feast of Weeks; agricultural festival associated with the giving of the law to Moses on Mount Sinai; occasion of the giving of the Holy Spirit to the first disciples.

Peter: one of the first disciples to be called by Jesus; originally called Simon but given the name 'Peter' ('Rock') by Jesus; fisherman, leader and spokesman for the disciples; denied Jesus; first leader of the early Church; died in 64–66 CE.

Pharisees: 'separated'; most influential group in Jerusalem at the time of Jesus; joined with other religious groups to plot the downfall of Jesus.

Pontius Pilate: procurator of Judea between 26 and 36 CE who had little time for his Jewish subjects; responsible for condemning Jesus to death; contemporary documents show him to have been a ruthless person.

prophet: person given a special task to perform for God and empowered by God's Spirit for this task.

Prophets: *see* Nevi'im.

Q

Qur'an: Muslim holy book; record of revelations given by Allah to Muhammad the Prophet.

R

rabbi: 'teacher'; man specially trained to teach the Jewish law and sacred writings; title occasionally applied to Jesus although he was not rabbinically trained.

Reformation: 16th-century movement for reform of certain doctrines and practices in the Roman Catholic Church which led to formation of several new Christian Churches.

Renaissance: period which saw the revival of art and literature in Europe from the 14th to the 16th centuries.

Roman Catholic Church: largest Christian Church worldwide; claims to have been founded by the apostle Peter; led by the Pope.

S

Sabbath day: 'cessation from work'; weekly day of rest in the Jewish community; Jesus had an ambivalent attitude towards the day; the early Church replaced it with Sunday, the day of resurrection, as their holy day.

sacrament: visible signs which Jesus commanded the Church to observe, such as baptism and the Lord's Supper, plus other signs which have a traditional place in Church worship but are not referred to in the Bible.

Sadducees: Jewish religious group at the time of Jesus; sometimes combined with the Pharisees, although the two groups were not friendly; believed in a policy of cooperation with the Romans.

Sanhedrin: 'council of leaders'; made up of 71 religious leaders; given religious responsibility within the confines of the holy city of Jerusalem.

Satan: Hebrew meaning 'accuser'; played a major part in the book of Job; leader of the angels opposed to God in the New Testament; tempted Jesus straight after his baptism.

Sermon on the Mount: title usually given to the teachings of Jesus gathered together in Matthew 5–7; includes the Beatitudes and practical instruction in almsgiving, prayer and fasting.

Shavout: Jewish Feast of Weeks; celebrated 50 days after Passover; commemorates the giving of the law to Moses on Mount Sinai.

Shema: 'hear'; first Hebrew word of the fundamental statement of Jewish belief in the oneness of God taken from Deuteronomy 6:4; Jesus called it the first commandment of the law.

Simeon: devout old man who delivered two prophecies about the infant Jesus, one of which is known as the Nunc Dimittis.

Son of man: preferred title of Jesus for himself; emphasizes the humanity and humiliation of Jesus; strongly linked to the ruler of the coming kingdom of God.

stations of the cross: 14 sculptures or paintings around the outside walls of Roman Catholic churches illustrating places where Jesus stopped on the way to his crucifixion.

Sukkot: 'booths'; Jewish autumn festival known also as Tabernacles.

Synagogue: 'meeting together'; meeting place for Jews living outside Jerusalem; place for study and fellowship apart from worship.

Synoptic Gospels: 'looking together'; title applied to the Gospels of Matthew, Mark and Luke which have much material in common and take a similar approach to the life of Jesus.

T

Tabernacles: Jewish harvest festival; Jews live in temporary shelters during the week to remind them of the journey of the Jews through the wilderness.

Talmud: major source of Jewish law; made up of oral laws and rabbinic commentaries.

tefillin: black leather boxes containing passages from the scriptures; worn on the arm and forehead; also called phylacteries.

Temple: three successive Temples were built in Jerusalem, the most important being the first built by Solomon and the third started by

Herod the Great; Herod's Temple was destroyed by the Romans in 70 CE.

Ten Commandments: series of 10 instructions which God inscribed on two tablets of stone for Moses on Mount Sinai; sometimes called the Decalogue; at the heart of the Jewish law.

tetrarch: subordinate ruler in Roman times; two of Herod the Great's sons, Philip and Antipas, were made tetrarchs over certain portions of their father's kingdom after his death.

Torah: the Law; the first five books of the Jewish scriptures: Genesis, Exodus, Leviticus, Deuteronomy and Numbers; laid the foundations for the way that Jews were expected to live.

transfiguration: the changing of Jesus' appearance before three disciples on a mountain; a reminder of the divine nature of Jesus.

Trinity: one God in three persons – God the Father, God the Son and God the Holy Spirit.

V

Via Dolorosa: 'Way of Sorrows'; path that Jesus is believed to have followed from the judgment hall of Pilate to his place of execution.

virgin birth: Christian belief that Jesus was born to a virgin, Mary, and conceived by the Holy Spirit and not a human father.

Virgin Mary: mother of Jesus Christ; object of devotion by Roman Catholic Christians.

W

Writings: *see* Ketuvim.

Z

Zechariah: father of John the Baptist; elderly priest struck dumb when his wife, Elizabeth, told him she was going to have a baby.

Picture Acknowledgments

The Art Archive: pp. 16, 110 (*Jesus Christ at Supper with Simon the Pharisee* [fresco, 1072]: Basilica San Angelo in Formis, Capua, Italy/Dagli Orti).

Julie Baines: p. 41.

Bible Society: p. 150 (© 1980 ITC Entertainment Ltd).

The Board of Trinity College, Dublin: p. 31 (*Book of Kells*, fol. 27v).

Bodleian Library, University of Oxford: p. 3 (ms. Auct. T. inf. 1.10, fol. 178v), 26–27 (roll 181 A [8], 8.26), 32 (ms. Auct. T. inf. 1.10, fol. 80v), 34 (ms. Auct. T. inf. 1.10, fol. 23v), 35 (ms. Auct. T. inf. 1.10, fol. 118v), 39 (ms. Auct. T. inf. 1.10, fol. 178v), 44 (Keble College, ms. 49, fol. 239), 55 (ms. Rawl. Liturg. f. 26, fol. 7r–169v, fol. 83v), 63 (Corpus Christi College, ms. 410, fol. 40), 67 (Corpus Christi College, ms. 410, fol. 47), 71 (ms. Junius 11, the Caedmon manuscript, fol. 3), 86 (ms. douce 311, fol. 8v), 130 (ms. douce 14, fol. 129v), 135 (ms. Gough liturg. 2, fol. 31), 143 (Corpus Christi College, ms. 410 [ministry of Christ], fol. 58v).

Bridgeman Art Library: pp. 6 (*The Road to Jerusalem* [panel] by Fra Angelico [Guido di Pietro] [c. 1387–1455]: Museo di San Marco dell'Angelico, Florence, Italy), 40 (aurcus [obverse] of Nero [54–68 CE] wearing a laurel wreath; inscription: NERO CAESAR AVGVSTVS [gold] by Roman [first century CE]: private collection), 47 (Deesis Christ with St John the Baptist [detail, mosaic]: Hagia Sophia, Istanbul, Turkey), 58 (ms. 36–1950, fol. 49v, *Christ Among the Apostles*, from a psalter possibly made for the Duchess of Breslau, mid-13th century [vellum]: Fitzwilliam Museum, University of Cambridge, UK), 64 (*The Miraculous Draught of Fishes* [cartoon for the Sistine Chapel, pre-restoration] by Raphael [Raffaello Sanzio of Urbino] [1483–1520]: Victoria and Albert Museum, London, UK), 78–79 (*The Last Supper* by Fra Angelico [Guido di Pietro] [c. 1387–1455]: Museo di San Marco dell'Angelico, Florence, Italy), 82–83 (*Last Judgment*, altarpiece from Santa Maria degli Angioli [panel, c. 1431] by Fra Angelico [Guido di Pietro] [c. 1387–1455]: Museo di San Marco dell'Angelico, Florence, Italy), 90–91 (*The Sermon on the Mount* [fresco, 1442] by Fra Angelico [Guido di Pietro] [c. 1387–1455]: Museo di San Marco dell'Angelico, Florence, Italy), 96 (Add. 47682, *Christ Calling His Apostles and Disciples* [vellum] by the English School [14th century] Holkham Bible [1327–35]: British Library, London, UK), 113 (*The Road to Jerusalem* [panel] by Fra Angelico [Guido di Pietro] [c. 1387–1455]: Museo di San Marco dell'Angelico, Florence, Italy), 123 (*Road to Calvary* by Simone Martini [1284–1344]: Musée du Louvre, Paris, France), 132–33 (*The Adoration of the Lamb* [lower half of central panel, 1425–32] by Jan van Eyck [c. 1390–1441]: St Bavo Cathedral, Ghent, Belgium), 153 (*Head of Christ* [pencil and wash] by Leonardo da Vinci [1452–1519]: Pinacoteca di Brera, Milan, Italy).

The British Library: p. 89 (*Haggadah Shil Pesach*, Or. 1404, fol. 7v). By permission of The British Library.

The British Museum: pp. 14, 147.

Estate of Yigael Yadin: p. 20.

Jewish Museum, London: p. 144 (*The Plunder of the Ghetto Following the Fettmilch Riots in August 1614* by H. Merian).

John Rylands Library: p. 38 (bottom).

Jon Arnold Images: pp. 8–9, 18.

Alex Keene (The Walking Camera): pp. 5, 21, 53, 81, 121, 148.

Lion Publishing: pp. 2 (right), 2–3 (David Townsend), 4–5 (David Townsend), 10 (middle right and bottom right), 10 (bottom left, David Townsend), 11 (both, David Townsend), 12 (David Townsend), 13 (both, David Townsend), 15 (David Townsend), 16–17 (David Townsend), 17 (David Townsend), 18 (David Townsend), 22–23 (David Townsend), 25 (David Townsend), 28 (David Townsend), 50 (David Townsend), 62 (David Townsend), 73 (David Townsend), 104, 107 (David Townsend), 108 (David Townsend), 128 (David Townsend), 136–37 (© Benedettine di Priscilla).

The National Gallery, London: pp. 49 (*The Annunciation* by Duccio di Buoninsegna [c. 1255–c. 1318]), 51 (*The Adoration of the Shepherds* [Italian, Neapolitan, c. 1630]), 54–55 (*The Adoration of the Kings*, attributed to Zanobi Strozzi [1412–68]), 57 (*The Circumcision* by Giovanni Bellini [c. 1430–1516]), 77 (*The Raising of Lazarus* [detail] by Sebastiano del Piombo [c. 1485–1547]), 95 (*The Agony in the Garden* by Giovanni Bellini [c. 1430–1516]), 124 (*Head of Christ Crucified* by the Master of Liesborn [active during second half of 15th century]), 129 (*The Incredulity of Saint Thomas* by Giovanni Battista Cima de Coñegliano [c. 1459–c. 1518]), 138–39 (*The Adoration of the Shepherds* by Guido Reni [1575–1642]).

Photo Scala, Florence: pp. 85 (*The Lost Drachma* by Domenico Feti [1589–1624]: Galleria Palatina, Firenze), 127 (*The Lamentation Before the Tomb* by Rogier van der Weyden [c. 1399–1464]), 142 (*The Three Marys at the Sepulchre* by Annibale Carracci [1560–1609]: Museo dell'Ermitage, St Petersburg, Russia).

Nicholas Rous: p. 38 (top).

Superstock: pp. 2 (left, *The Betrayal of Jesus* [detail from the Maestà altarpiece] by Duccio di Buoninsegna [c. 1255–c. 1318]: Museo dell'Opera del Duomo, Siena, Italy/Canali Photobank, Milan), 42–43 (*The Finding of the Saviour in the Temple* by William Holman Hunt [1827–1910]: Birmingham City Gallery & Museum, England), 61 (*Baptism of Christ* by the Master of Female Half-Lengths [active 1500–30]: Christie's Images), 68 (*Healing the Woman with the Issue of Blood* by Veronese [Paolo Caliari] [1528–88]), 74–75 (*The Storm on the Sea of Galilee* by Rembrandt van Rijn [1606–69]: Isabella Stewart Gardner Museum, Boston, Massachusetts), 93 (*Healing of the Ten Lepers* by James Tissot [1836–1902]), 99 (*Eternal Image* [1998] by Serguei Orgunov: Krasnaya), 100–101 (*The Creation of Man* by Marc Chagall [1887–1985]: Musée de Biblique, Nice, © 2001 ADAGP, Paris and DACS, London), 102 (*They Cast Stones at Him* by James Tissot [1836–1902]), 109 (*The Transfiguration of Our Lord* [14th-century Russian icon]: Leonid Bogdanov), 115 (*Last Supper* [mural]: church in Goreme, Turkey/Silvio Fiore), 116 (*The Betrayal of Jesus* [detail from the Maestà altarpiece] by Duccio di Buoninsegna [c. 1255–c. 1318]: Museo dell'Opera del Duomo, Siena, Italy/Canali Photobank, Milan), 118–19 (*Calvary* [c. 1457–60] by Andrea Mantegna [1431–1506]: Musée du Louvre, Paris), 120 (*Jesus Before Caiaphas* by Giotto di Bondone [c. 1267–1337]: Arena Chapel, Cappella degli Scrovegni, Padua, Italy), 141 (*The Crucifixion* by Jacopo Tintoretto [1518–94]: Civic Museum, Padua, Italy), 149 (*The Last Supper* by Elimo Njau).

Derek West: front endpaper, pp. 11, 36.